EXPERIENCING LED ZEPPELIN

The Listener's Companion
Gregg Akkerman, Series Editor

Titles in **The Listener's Companion** provide readers with a deeper understanding of key musical genres and the work of major artists and composers. Aimed at nonspecialists, each volume explains in clear and accessible language how to listen to works from particular artists, composers, and genres. Looking at both the context in which the music first appeared and has since been heard, authors explore with readers the environments in which key musical works were written and performed.

Experiencing Jazz: A Listener's Companion, by Michael Stephans
Experiencing Led Zeppelin: A Listener's Companion, by Gregg Akkerman
Experiencing Mozart: A Listener's Companion, by David Schroeder
Experiencing Rush: A Listener's Companion, by Durrell Bowman
Experiencing Stravinsky: A Listener's Companion, by Robin Maconie
Experiencing Verdi: A Listener's Companion, by Donald Sanders

EXPERIENCING LED ZEPPELIN

A Listener's Companion

Gregg Akkerman

ROWMAN & LITTLEFIELD
Lanham • Boulder • New York • London

Published by Rowman & Littlefield
A wholly owned subsidiary of The Rowman & Littlefield Publishing Group,
Inc.
4501 Forbes Boulevard, Suite 200, Lanham, Maryland 20706
www.rowman.com

16 Carlisle Street, London W1D 3BT, United Kingdom

British Library Cataloguing in Publication Information Available

Library of Congress Cataloging-in-Publication Data

Akkerman, Gregg.
Experiencing Led Zeppelin : a listener's companion / Gregg Akkerman.
pages cm. — (The listener's companion)
Includes bibliographical references and index.
ISBN 978-0-8108-8915-6 (cloth : alk. paper) – ISBN 978-0-8108-8916-3 (ebook : alk. paper)
1. Led Zeppelin (Musical group) 2. Rock music–1971–1980–History and criticism. 3. Rock music–1961–1970–History and criticism. I. Title.
ML421.L4A45 2014
782.42166092'2–dc23
2014017048

♾ ™ The paper used in this publication meets the minimum requirements of
American National Standard for Information Sciences Permanence of Paper
for Printed Library Materials, ANSI/NISO Z39.48-1992.

Printed in the United States of America

CONTENTS

ACKNOWLEDGMENTS

- Jack Hansen for the floating hideout.
- Alex Shayne for the clarity.
- Dave Akkerman for playing the right records.
- Elgé Davis for the cymbal crash.
- Elsa Jensen for the licorice.
- Nathan Hubbard for the drum beat.
- Bennett Graff for the green light.
- MJ Akkerman for the calm.

TIMELINE

January 9, 1944	James (Jimmy) Patrick Page born in Heston, Middlesex, England.
January 3, 1946	James Baldwin (John Paul Jones) born in Sidcup, Kent, England.
May 31, 1948	John Henry Bonham born in Redditch, Worcestershire, England.
August 20, 1948	Robert Anthony Plant born in West Bromwich, Staffordshire, England.
June 1966	Jimmy Page joins the Yardbirds
December 1966	John Paul Jones arranges the strings for the song "Little Games" recorded by the Yardbirds.
March 1967	Robert Plant and John Bonham play together in the Band of Joy.
July 7, 1968	Final performance of the Yardbirds with Jimmy Page.
September 1968	Rehearsals begin for the New Yardbirds with Jimmy Page, Robert Plant, John Paul Jones, and John Bonham managed by Peter Grant.
September 7, 1968	The New Yardbirds play their first performance at the Gladsaxe Teen Club

	in Egegardaskolen, Gladsaxe, Denmark. They are paid 7,000 Danish Kroner.
October 1968	Recording sessions for the album *Led Zeppelin* at Olympic Studios in Barnes, England.
October 17, 1968	First performance using the name "Led Zeppelin" at Surrey University, England.
November, 1968	Manager Peter Grant arranges a record deal for Led Zeppelin with Atlantic Records, who would remain the band's only distributor.
December 26, 1968	First American show in Boston, Massachusetts.
January 12, 1969	The album *Led Zeppelin* released in America.
October 17, 1969	The first rock band to perform at Carnegie Hall.
October 22, 1969	The album *Led Zeppelin II* released in America.
May 1970	Robert Plant and Jimmy Page visit the Welsh cottage known as Bron-Yr-Aur to write music.
October 5, 1970	The album *Led Zeppelin III* released in America.
November 8, 1971	Led Zeppelin's fourth album (untitled) released in America.
March 28, 1973	The album *Houses of the Holy* released in America.
May 5, 1973	Led Zeppelin performs a concert at the Tampa Stadium to an audience of 56,800.
July 29, 1973	The band robbed of over $200,000 in cash at the Drake Hotel in New York City.
May 10, 1974	The band launches their record company, Swan Song.

February 24, 1975   The album *Physical Graffiti* released in America.

August 4, 1975   Robert Plant injured in an automobile accident while in Rhodes, Greece.

March 31, 1976   The album *Presence* released in America.

October 20, 1976   The movie *The Song Remains the Same* released in America. The double-album soundtrack also released.

July 23, 1977   Band crew and John Bonham involved with a backstage beating in Oakland, California.

July 26, 1977   Robert Plant's son Karac dies while band is in America. Tour canceled and Plant returns to England.

August 4, 1979   The band plays their last engagement in their homeland at Knebworth, England.

August 15, 1979   The album *In Through the Out Door* released in America.

October 27, 1979   The entire Led Zeppelin album catalog appears on the *Billboard* Top 200 chart during the same week.

July 7, 1980   The band plays their final performance with all original members in Eissporthalle, Berlin, Germany.

September 25, 1980   John Bonham dies at the home of Jimmy Page after a night of heavy drinking.

December 4, 1980   The band announces their break-up. The official Led Zeppelin press release reads: "We wish it to be known, that the loss of our dear friend and the deep respect we have for his family, together with the deep sense of undivided harmony felt by ourselves and our manager, have led us to decide that we could not continue as we were."

June 28, 1982   Robert Plant releases *Pictures at Eleven*,
                             his first solo album: the only Plant solo
                             album released on the Swan Song label.

November 19, 1982   The Led Zeppelin album *Coda* released
                             in America. This was one of the last
                             releases on the Swan Song label started
                             by Led Zeppelin.

September 21, 1983   The first post-Zeppelin concert
                             appearance by Jimmy Page and he
                             performed an instrumental version of
                             "Stairway to Heaven."

February 11, 1985   *The Firm* album released by Jimmy Page
                             with vocalist Paul Rogers.

July 13, 1985   The three surviving members of Led
                             Zeppelin perform with Phil Collins on
                             drums for the U.S. Live Aid concert held
                             at the JFK Stadium in Philadelphia.

May 14, 1988   The three surviving members of Led
                             Zeppelin perform with John Bonham's
                             son Jason on drums for the Atlantic
                             Records fortieth anniversary concert.

June 19, 1988   Jimmy Page releases first solo album,
                             Outrider, on Geffen Records.

September 1988   Jimmy Page tours in support of his
                             Outrider album with Jason Bonham on
                             drums.

April 28, 1990   The three surviving members of Led
                             Zeppelin perform with Jason Bonham at
                             his wedding reception.

September 7, 1990   The boxed set *Led Zeppelin* with fifty-
                             four digitally remastered tracks is released
                             worldwide.

March 15, 1993   Vocalist David Coverdale and Jimmy
                             Page release the album *Coverdale-Page*
                             on Geffen Records.

September 21, 1993   The remainder of the Led Zeppelin album catalog is digitally remastered and released as *Led Zeppelin Boxed Set 2.*

Autumn 1994   Jimmy Page and Robert Plant perform for MTV's *Unplugged* before embarking on an extensive tour featuring many Led Zeppelin songs and the release of the album *No Quarter: Unledded.*

January 12, 1995   Led Zeppelin inducted into the Rock and Roll Hall of Fame.

January 31, 1995   Led Zeppelin presented the American Music Awards "International Artist Award."

November 21, 1995   Peter Grant, Led Zeppelin's only manager, dies at age 60.

May 29, 1997   Led Zeppelin presented the Ivor Novello Lifetime Achievement Award for songwriting.

November 11, 1997   The Led Zeppelin album *BBC Sessions* released in America.

February 25, 1998   Robert Plant and Jimmy Page awarded a Grammy for Best Hard Rock Performance ("Most High").

April 21, 1998   Robert Plant and Jimmy Page release the album *Walking into Clarksdale* on Atlantic Records.

February 24, 1999   *Led Zeppelin IV* inducted into the Grammy Hall of Fame.

February 23, 2003   "Stairway to Heaven" inducted into the Grammy Hall of Fame.

May 26, 2003   The *Led Zeppelin DVD* released featuring several concert films.

May 27, 2003	The album *How the West Was Won* released featuring live concerts recorded in 1972.
February 8, 2004	*Led Zeppelin* (the album) inducted into the Grammy Hall of Fame.
February 13, 2005	Led Zeppelin presented with the Grammy Lifetime Achievement Award.
May 22, 2006	Led Zeppelin awarded the Polar Music Prize (Sweden), which includes a stipend of 1 million Swedish Kroner.
November 14, 2006	Led Zeppelin inducted into the United Kingdom Music Hall of Fame to acknowledge their worldwide sales of over 300 million records.
February 11, 2007	Robert Plant (with Alison Krauss) awarded Grammy for Best Pop Collaboration with Vocals for the song "Gone Gone Gone (Done Moved On)."
November 2007	Led Zeppelin is one of the last major rock bands to release their catalog as digital downloads.
November 13, 2007	The compilation album *Mothership* released in America featuring twenty-four recordings.
December 10, 2007	The three surviving members of Led Zeppelin perform with Jason Bonham on drums at a full-length concert commemorating the life of Atlantic Records executive Ahmet Ertegun at the O2 Arena in London, England.
February 11, 2008	"Whole Lotta Love" inducted into the Grammy Hall of Fame.
June 16, 2008	Led Zeppelin awarded "Best Live Act" by *Mojo Magazine*.

September 3, 2008	Led Zeppelin presented the Outstanding Achievement Award from *GQ Magazine*.
February 10, 2008	Robert Plant (with Alison Krauss) awarded five Grammys: Record of the Year ("Please Read the Letter" written by Plant and Jimmy Page); Album of the Year (*Raising Sand*); Best Pop Collaboration with Vocals ("Rich Woman"); Best Country Collaboration with Vocals ("Killing the Blues"); Best Contemporary Folk/Americana Album (*Raising Sand*).
December 16, 2009	Guinness Book of World Records confirms that Led Zeppelin broke the world record for the "Highest Demand for Tickets for One Music Concert" when 20 million requests came through for the one-time reunion show in December 2007.
November 19, 2012	The film and album *Celebration Day* released featuring the 2007 concert at the O2 Arena.
December 2, 2012	Led Zeppelin acknowledged by President Obama at the Kennedy Center Honors.
March 21, 2013	Led Zeppelin receives the Echo Award (Germany) for "International Lifetime Achievement."
January 26, 2014	*Celebration Day* is awarded the Grammy for Best Rock Album. "Kashmir" from the same album is nominated for "Best Rock Performance."
2014–2015	The release (one album at a time) of the entire Led Zeppelin catalog digitally remastered for the first time since the 1993 boxed sets, all produced by Jimmy Page. Each album includes a collection of

bonus material including outtakes, alternate takes, live recordings, or alternate mixes.

INTRODUCTION
Time to Change the Road You're On

Led Zeppelin was not created from nothing. They are not divine. Their roots are as pedestrian as any British band from the late 1960s hoping to get a song on the radio and travel around Europe so they could meet girls and put off having to get proper jobs for as long as possible. England was full of many one-hit wonders like the Honeycombs, the Silkie, and Whistling Jack Smith. Who was to say in 1968 that Led Zeppelin wouldn't become just another footnote on the British charts? Was there really something different about these four lads? In a word: absolutely.

One substantial difference was that these particular bandmates were exceptionally good musicians. Such a thing was not a given for bands of the period, who often didn't play instruments on their own albums. In fact, two members of Led Zeppelin had made their living as session musicians often called upon to buttress the performance weaknesses of the hit-makers of the day. The guitarist was a new breed of six-string gunslinger with vision and experience well beyond his years. The vocalist was blues drenched and blessed with a voice like no one else before him. The drummer had thunderous power and a machine-like groove. The bassist could double on the keyboard and wrote riffs as infectious as they were complex. And it wouldn't hurt that they were all devilishly handsome and had a manager both tough and smart enough to keep them in demand while protecting their brand. But their coalescence was not unwarranted happenstance. Proactive decisions were made.

Luck was forged from opportunistic risks. These five men each brought their individual skills, failings, hopes, and personalities to the mix before the gods hammered out the kinks on what would eventually become a hard-rock mother ship with a profound and lasting shadow.

THE MANAGER

Peter Grant was born April 5, 1935, making him nearly nine years older than any member of Led Zeppelin. To a twenty-year-old aspiring rock musician, Grant, only in his late twenties, was already a rock-industry veteran who had traveled the world. He first dipped his toe in artistic waters as an actor, earning small roles in movies like *Guns of Navarone* and *Cleopatra*. Despite the minor on-screen credits, he found himself making more money transporting bands between performance venues, and this led to his being hired by Don Arden as a tour manager. Grant's early charges included rock pioneers like Bo Diddley, Little Richard, and Chuck Berry. This experience eventually allowed Grant to begin managing acts on his own through an office shared with the well-known music manager/producer Mickie Most. Grant's imposing physical size and adamant stance that the musicians he represented would be paid well and on time began to fuel his lifelong reputation as a difficult and even brutish man to work with. Grant found that such a reputation, even if often exaggerated, was a powerful negotiation tool, and he did little to dispel it. It was hoped that Grant could apply his growing skill set to rekindle the fading career of the Yardbirds with an exuberant Jimmy Page on guitar. The attempts to save the group from their fate came too late, but Grant increased his managerial prowess during their English and American tours, and this would pay off in later years with both Led Zeppelin and Bad Company. When Page began to describe the post-Yardbirds endeavor he was hoping to form in 1968, Grant was keen enough to see the potential in the guitarist's proposal and set about to assist in filling the roster for a new band.

THE DRUMMER

Born in 1948, John Bonham has often been named the greatest of all rock drummers, and he achieved that title without ever seeing his thirty-third birthday. His lightning-fast footwork and creative fills are a matter of record, but what he had that was lacking in many of his contemporaries is less tangible. His sense of "groove" has seldom been matched. It can't be easily measured and held up for obvious comparison, but you know it when you hear it, and groove is heard throughout the Zeppelin catalog. Perhaps it was due to Bonham's unteachable ability to know when to play less when those around him played more. It might also have been because he could dig in and hit his drums with punishing intensity. The secret to the Bonham groove might even be related to his larger-than-life persona and the angst he let loose on tour to compensate for missing his family.

Bonham, known affectionately by his Zeppelin bandmates as "Bonzo," began playing drums as a teenager and although he had no formal music training, he found early inspiration in jazz greats Gene Krupa and Buddy Rich. Out of school, Bonham played in a string of pub bands while continuing to work day shifts as a carpenter. He married young and found supporting his new wife, Pat, exclusively through music to be an ongoing challenge. One of the many bands Bonham traveled in and out of was the Crawling King Snakes, who had a little-known vocalist named Robert Plant. The two struck up a friendship and later recorded together in another unsuccessful outfit named the Band of Joy. Bonham finally found regular income playing in the backing band for American Tim Rose while he toured Britain in 1968. It was during this time that a request arrived through his mate Plant regarding a new band that had something to do with the Yardbirds. Bonham wasn't convinced. He had a steady gig that didn't require him to stray too far from Pat. Why give that up for yet another Robert Plant scheme when the first two hadn't gotten them anywhere?

THE BASSIST

James Baldwin was born in 1946 to parents who were active musicians and encouraged him to play piano at a young age. He is the only member of Led Zeppelin to study music formally, and as a teenager he performed as a church organist about the same time he acquired a bass guitar. By the age of sixteen he was good enough on the new instrument to play professionally with former members of the Shadows, who referred him to studio session work for Decca Records. Baldwin soon found all the work he could handle as a bassist, keyboardist, and arranger. He adopted the professional name of John Paul Jones (taken from a French movie of the same name), and his credits included work with the Rolling Stones, Jeff Beck, Donovan, Herman's Hermits, and Rod Stewart. Eventually, Jones's path crossed that of Jimmy Page, who also worked constantly in the early 1960s as a session player, and the two agreed that they would be interested in working together. After the split of the Yardbirds, Jones's wife suggested he give Page a call to see if the time was right for collaboration. Jones was exhausted from the grind of session dates and thought touring around for a while would be a nice break. Page had at first reached out to Yardbirds bassist Chris Dreja but saw potential in working with a schooled and disciplined musician like Jones. With a bassist in hand, Page could now focus on finding the right vocalist.

THE SINGER

Robert Plant was born in August 1948, making him the youngest member of Led Zeppelin (Bonham was only three months older). Leaving home at the hard-to-conceive young age of sixteen, Plant grew up fast and embraced the blues-singing lifestyle of his "teachers": Howlin' Wolf, Willie Dixon, and Robert Johnson. He befriended Bonham when they both played for a spell in the Crawling King Snakes, and Plant even had a brief recording career as a teenager with CBS Records. The singles he released proved unsuccessful and Plant still worked odd jobs such as laying pavement while he moved through other bands, including the Band of Joy and Hobbstweedle. It was while with the latter that Page came to hear him sing and was quick to offer Plant a chance to join a new group. Page mentioned he was still looking for a drummer, and Plant immediately suggested his mate Bonham, who was only convinced to join in the foray after several telegrams. Just past his twentieth birthday, Plant was about to begin his march toward becoming the greatest voice hard rock had ever heard.

THE GUITARIST

Jimmy Page is the oldest member of Led Zeppelin, born in January 1944. Growing up around London, Page began teaching himself to play guitar at age 12 by listening to records featuring such mentors as Scotty Moore, Hubert Sumlin, and Buddy Guy. Page was already skilled enough on guitar by age 13 to make an appearance on BBC1 television playing skiffle music. By age 15, he began a two-year stint performing with Neil Christian and the Crusaders, but a recurring case of glandular fever eventually took him out of action. As was the case with so many British rock musicians in the 1960s, Page attended art college but played music in bands part time and often crossed paths with guitarists Jeff Beck and Eric Clapton at London nightclubs like the Marquee. The three men would eventually be considered the Holy Trinity of British rock guitarists. By 1963, Page had found himself in demand as a recording session musician, often beefing up the guitar parts for bands that were weak in that area. Over the next three years, Page played on records for artists like the Kinks, the Who, Van Morrison, the Rolling Stones, Donovan, and Joe Cocker, as well as hundreds of now-forgotten sessions that paid the bills but offered little artistic satisfaction.

By 1966, Page felt the need for a change and jumped at the chance to play with his mate Jeff Beck in the Yardbirds, even though it meant his having to play bass, an instrument he had never played. It wasn't long before Page traded places with the rhythm guitar player, and for a short time the Yardbirds featured two of Britain's best guitarists in the same band. While touring America, the temperamental Beck left the group, allowing Page to become a stronger force in the band, choosing their material and becoming more particular about their recordings. Despite his best efforts, the rest of the Yardbirds had grown weary of traveling and, finding less success at home in England, called a halt to the band in July 1968.

Page had gotten a taste of having his own band traveling to America and playing music—that was consistently more fulfilling than session work. While in the Yardbirds he had found a manager in Peter Grant, who Page knew could be trusted, and the two agreed that another band should be formed to satisfy some contracted gigs still on the calendar. John Paul Jones was as solid as they came and had already agreed to play bass anytime Page was ready. Grant and Page had taken the time to hear Robert Plant sing and could hardly believe no one had snatched him up beforehand. And with Plant's recommendation for drummer John Bonham, who played as hard and loud as any they had ever heard, the stars finally aligned. Jimmy Page had a new band ready to make music.

THE BAND

Page, Plant, Jones, and Bonham all rehearsed together for the first time in September 1968. The first song they played was "Train Kept A-Rollin'," and the reaction of the four was immediate. The room crackled with energy, and they knew something special had happened. The four hastily began organizing a music set so they could play dates that October as the New Yardbirds. Since time was short, they leaned heavily on blues numbers and songs Page had already been developing in his days with the old Yardbirds. Jones contributed riffs for "Good Times, Bad Times," and Plant came up with some original lyrics, even though a previously signed publishing agreement kept him from receiving credit as lyricist on their first album.

After solidifying their set by playing these first few concert dates, the band entered Olympic Recording Studios in October 1968 and captured on tape a rendition of their live show. Add to this their newly adopted name, which most likely came from The Who's John Entwistle (although Keith Moon tried to take credit), and Led Zeppelin emerged as a band with a brand and a completed album. Manager Peter Grant could now work his magic and set the group's trajectory toward unknown heights.

THIS BOOK

I am a Led Zeppelin fan but not a Led Zeppelin fanatic. I do not know the specific guitar used by Page on every track. I do not own every bootleg recording. And I will never commit to memory the names of any of their pets. I am not their "biggest" fan, but I am a lifelong follower who still recalls feeling the immense excitement of bringing a new Zeppelin album home from the drug store (kids weren't always welcome in the local record stores, which at the time often doubled as drug paraphernalia shops). Lying on the shag carpet, I blissed out as I listened to each song for the first time and believed to my core that I was on the receiving end of a personal connection with the band. In the pre-Internet days of 1980, when news traveled slowly to small towns, I remember with horror reading in the local paper the all-too-brief article announcing the death of John Bonham. I still have the clipping. In college, I engaged in actual fisticuffs with a drunken partygoer who refused to recant or even defend his opinion that "Zeppelin sucked." Years later in graduate school I borrowed ideas from "Kashmir" and "In the Light" and incorporated them into formal compositions, much to the angst of my professors. While employed as a church pianist, I regularly slipped excerpts of "The Rain Song," "Going to California," and "That's the Way" into the accompaniment during meditations. And when Zeppelin announced a one-off reunion concert in 2007, I was one of the millions who failed at procuring a ticket.

So while I will always be a hyper-dedicated fan, I am not a Zeppelin apologist who will defend them against all charges. There are times they transcend all precedents ("Since I've Been Loving You") and times they spectacularly fail (the movie *The Song Remains the Same* is a case in point), so I have no problem identifying either. One particularly pleasing aspect to their music is how well it has weathered the passing of the decades. Jimmy Page is a creative guitarist but as a producer, the man is an absolute genius. There may be the occasional song or even album that you may not personally like, but it won't be because the audio sounded like crap. Few other bands of Zeppelin's era can make the same claim about the totality of their catalog. Jeff Beck played some amazing music on those early recordings with Rod Stewart, but I can barely tolerate the thin sound of the guitar, and the mix of the instruments could sometimes be a complete mess. The band Montrose got the guitar right but, try as they did, the drums on "Rock Candy" were just a poor man's imitation of "When the Levee Breaks." On the first couple of Black Sabbath albums Tony Iommi and Ozzy Osbourne still knock me out, but you don't hear anyone in a recording studio asking their producer to please give them that "War Pigs" snare drum sound. Say what you will about the absurdity of the Zeppelin mystique or the sometimes self-indulgent three-hour concerts, there is no opining that the overall sound of their albums sucked. I threw punches over it once, and I'd gladly do it again.

The contents of this book are laid out in chronological order. The fact that Zeppelin released nine studio albums during their active years lends itself nicely to the *Listener's Companion* series by assigning each album its own chapter. I also include *Coda* as one of the nine because even though it was released after Bonham's death, all of the music was supposedly recorded during his time in the band. Zeppelin's live albums, on the other hand, are explored primarily to offer analytical comparisons to the studio recordings. Each chapter places the making of the related album into the context of the times, but this gesture should not be confused with band biography by other means. For comprehensive tales of the band's history, I have listed my favorite books in the selected readings.

The emphasis of each chapter is on the experience of listening to the music of Led Zeppelin. Consider me the voice whispering in your ear as you begin the playback on your media device. Every song from their nine albums is discussed, but within each chapter a few titles are given special attention under the subheading of "A Closer Look." For these focused song-vignettes, I delve further into the music and provide a detailed "under the hood" analysis of the music as understood in both their original and present settings. While it might have been pompous fun to fill pages dissecting rarely heard and nearly impossible-to-find outtakes or concert bootlegs, I limit the conversation to Zeppelin material easily available for purchase or accessible through websites like YouTube. My intention is to welcome all generations of Zeppelin fans rather than exclude those who are still getting to know the band's music.

So enjoy the ride.

I

BEGGARS AND THIEVES

Led Zeppelin originated as a grand vision of guitarist Jimmy Page, who was faced with the need to fulfill contracts booked by his previous band, the Yardbirds. Zeppelin came together as two pairs of musicians, a configuration that would have a lasting impact on their music and group dynamic. While Page and bassist John Paul Jones were already successful studio musicians in London, vocalist Robert Plant and drummer John Bonham hailed from the Black Country outlands of Birmingham, where their talents had yet to be fully measured. The quartet's first album, eponymously titled *Led Zeppelin*, was financed by Page and recorded in only thirty hours of studio time. Not surprisingly, it included several live vocal and instrumental takes with no overdubs or corrections.

In the light of such a compressed time table, the biggest problem confronting Zeppelin was a lack of developed songs worthy enough to make a good showing on both a concert stage and, more importantly, a new album. At their first rehearsal they had trouble picking even one song they all knew and finally settled on "Train Kept A-Rolling." This lack of common material didn't bode well. In order to expedite the set list shortcoming, the band turned to the blues and a couple of tunes Page had already been performing with the Yardbirds.

The recording sessions began September 27, 1968, after the band had only been together for less than three weeks. With only fifteen hours of rehearsal and a scant ten gigs performed, the band entered the studio with the plan to essentially record a live version of their concert set, leaving out obvious cover songs like "Train" and "For Your Love." With this down-and-dirty plan, it is remarkable how this album contained all of Led Zeppelin's trademark characteristics already intact and fully formed: heavy metal timbre, blues-based riffs, wailing vocals, acoustic folk influences, and high-quality audio production.

The first song on Led Zeppelin's first album is an immediate double-punch to the gut: "Good Times Bad Times." The first two notes are among the most recognizable in rock music and it only gets better from there. All the band members get a turn to shine on this one. Bonzo is killing it with his triple-hit kick drum, Jones brings the bass to the front row, Page presents a clinic on how to play a molten solo, and Plant takes it to the rafters. The background harmonies in the chorus are hopelessly dated to the late 1960s, but on the plus side there is the right amount of cowbell. For a complete guided listening experience to a live version of "Good Times Bad Times" performed in 2007, see the "Closer Look" section of chapter 10.

Had there never been a "Stairway to Heaven," "Babe I'm Gonna Leave You" would have ruled as the archetype Zeppelin ballad. It was rather cheeky of Zeppelin to place a ballad as only the second song on the album when slow tempos are usually placed further down the playlist. But Page knew what history has confirmed; a song this good shouldn't have to wait in the shadows. Like "Stairway," the introduction is played on acoustic guitar with rolling chords in same dark minor key. And also like "Stairway," the song builds toward a power-chord sequence filled with passion and energy. One aspect favoring "Babe" over "Stairway" is that Plant's lyric is a straightforward love letter of sadness and confusion rather than obscure poetry about hedgerows and shining white light. The out-of-tune last chord is annoying at first but after hearing it enough times, you wouldn't want it any other way. A beautiful woman is even more memorable when she makes no effort to hide a blemish.

The first blues-based song on *Led Zeppelin* is "You Shook Me" and the band sets the bar exceedingly high. In the late 1960s into the 1970s, rock bands treated the blues as a placement test that needed to be taken very seriously. There was a deep respect for the blues among British musicians and including a blues on a record was a standard-issue move. White bands playing the blues in later years were labeled as pandering, trite, or (kiss of death) derivative, but not so at the end of

1968 and Zeppelin fans are better for it. "You Shook Me" could hardly be slower or any better.

Jimmy Page "borrowed" the basic structure for "Dazed and Confused" and had performed a version with the Yardbirds enough times to know that there was unmined potential. With Zeppelin, he had found the horsepower to develop "Dazed" into a mind-bending psychedelic trek. Jones and Bonham were strong enough players to handle the change in tempo and Plant had vocal skills well beyond those of Keith Relf. So while it's true that Zeppelin didn't invent "Dazed" from scratch, they own it like no other. Put on some headphones, turn out the lights, sit in the dark, and get rocked as your imagination sails "for so long it's not true."

If you bought the *Led Zeppelin* album new in 1969, you probably would have been so blown away by the first four songs that the only option was to keep playing side 1. But eventually, you would have settled down enough to move to side 2 and the first song is "Your Time Is Gonna Come." If the album has a weak link, this is it. "Your Time" is not a bad song. In fact, the organ introduction is downright respectable, the chords are good, and the melody and lyrics start out with an attractive sense of melancholy. But when the boys take you to the chorus, the bottom falls out. To hear poor background vocals, and Plant's dull melody telling us repeatedly that our "time is gonna come" just doesn't live up to the promise of the verses. It's no wonder that Page veered away from conventional pop song-forms like the one on "Your Time" and they would seldom be heard on Zeppelin records.

It was typical for Page to have an acoustic guitar feature at some point in a Yardbirds concert and he carried the tradition over to Zeppelin. "Black Mountain Side" demonstrably states that Zeppelin is a band led by their guitarist. Setting aside two minutes in which the other three musicians are sidelined gives Page the space to educate fans that he is more than just a blues-based rocker. The man spent years practicing his craft as a complete guitarist capable of finger picking, alternate tunings, and complex time signatures, and he isn't embarrassed to share those hard-won skills. "Black Mountain Side" is not flashy and the album would be just as strong in the song's absence, but it set a precedent for acoustic features in later years that were not to be missed.

The word *swagger* is used a few times in this book to describe a mostly indescribable aspect of Page as a guitarist. There's just something about his rhythmic groove that sways and bends around the tempo in a loosely tight (or is that tightly loose?) manner. When seen in concert, his swagger is all the more evident, but on *Led Zeppelin* it can clearly be heard on "Communication Breakdown." Had Zeppelin only released this one song as a single and then quickly broken up, they still would have taken a sledgehammer to the future of guitarists all over the world who, upon hearing the song, shout out, "That's how I want to play!" Zeppelin did not invent hard rock or heavy metal, but they codified the parameters and formulated the mission statement for others to adopt as their own. It lasts less than 2:30, but that's all the time it takes for "Communication Breakdown" to change the road you're on.

The second blues on *Led Zeppelin* is "I Can't Quit You Baby" written by Willie Dixon. Like the most popular blues-based songs, "I Can't Quit You Baby" is based on a twelve-measure progression of chords that is repeated as necessary for verses and solos. The last two measures of the pattern feature a clever lift in the chords that creates tension and release but the idea came from Dixon. What is striking about this track is that it is recorded completely live with no overdubs. No extra guitars, background vocals, keyboards, or percussion are heard. Zeppelin plays it straight through and has the guts to leave it just the way it went down on tape. And they nailed it. "A Closer Look" at a live version of "I Can't Quit You Babe" is found in chapter 9.

"How Many More Times" closes out the album and, like "Dazed and Confused" on side 1, is a vehicle for Zeppelin to stretch out as songwriters and improvisers. Unlike the raw "live" quality of "I Can't Quit You Baby," the band takes the time here to orchestrate many textural layers and complex changes in rhythmic feel. Much more than end-of-the-album filler, this is epic rock and roll that cleared the path for later Zeppelin iconoclasts like "In the Light" and "In My Time of Dying."

A CLOSER LOOK

"Communication Breakdown"

You settle the needle in the groove of "Communication Breakdown" and are quickly knocked back by the guitar in full overdrive and making formidable use of the aggressive lowest-pitched string as Jimmy Page piles on with nine hammer blows in rapid succession followed immediately by three powerful chord hits. This crushing introduction from "Breakdown" on the second side of Led Zeppelin's first album laid down a new gauntlet in rock music that is still being responded to decades later. This song was the archetype for the emerging heavy-metal sound in the late 1960s and part of the reason Led Zeppelin is still regarded as a founding father of the genre. If any band now or in the future wants to rain down heavy-metal thunder, they could do no worse than conjuring their own version of "Breakdown."

During the second airing of the riff, the drums and bass join in for short, accented hits that support the guitar and build momentum toward the inevitable, energetic release of the caged rhythm Jimmy Page uses as bait to attract the listener. Mercifully, the instrumental trio begins the song in earnest on the fifth incarnation of the riff as John Bonham begins his classic, driving rock beat under the high-note entrance of Robert Plant's vocal: "Hey girl, stop what you're doing." The pop-song-marketing mentality of singers performing songs designed for group participation through easy melodies in the medium vocal range for nonprofessionals was shattered by the time Plant arrives at the word *girl*. He is not leading a campfire sing-along. Instead, he announces himself as a new breed of rock vocalist that belts out blues-based subject matter in an elevated range leaving the amateurs behind. Considering Plant's youth (age 20) at the time of this recording, you might be utterly amazed at his pure gall, or perhaps even offended by the same, but the one thing you likely cannot do is easily sing along. He is essentially saying, "Don't even bother mate—I've got this."

The vocal verses take place over eight repetitions of the opening riff before charging directly to the chorus without any transitional material. The chords finally move away from the home base but stay well within the traditional sonic landscape of the blues and feature a nice syncopation of unexpected rhythmic hits throughout the chorus. Plant's vocals take on a decidedly thicker tone at this point due to the technique called double tracking in which two different recordings of his voice are heard at the same time. The lyrics of the hook "I'm having a nervous breakdown, drive me insane" call out timelessly to disenfranchised youth and Plant further paints the picture by holding the word *insane* with a brief but wailing descent. To add further emphasis to this moment, the band pulls back by returning to the opening riff in which the guitar is heard by itself before the drums and bass rejoin. Thus, the flow of energy is brought back down, only to explode all over again for the second verse. As Plant calls out to a woman who has surely done him wrong, "I'm never gonna let you go, 'cause I like your charms," we are led to the next chorus, but this time the two vocal parts deviate. In traditional double tracking, there is an attempt to have the multiple recorded takes mimic each other as accurately as possible, as if to add to the overall volume of sound but not distract the listener by presenting conflicting versions of the melody. Not so on "Breakdown," where two distinct "Roberts" are heard singing simultaneously at the end of the second chorus. While one voice cuts off "insane" similar to the earlier chorus, a second drifts in seemingly pained suspension until reluctantly releasing the listener to the impending guitar solo on the word *suck*.

Page dominates the song at this point with a blistering and high-pitched opening to his guitar solo played over the riff used for the verse. And unlike pre–Led Zeppelin recordings of Page where the mixing choices were made by pop-minded, radio-friendly producers who view solos as something to quickly get out of the way between vocals, this lead work is placed unapologetically in the forefront as a featured component. Led Zeppelin is announcing in "Breakdown" that they are a band featuring not only an incredible singer, but also a guitarist of rare talent that will not be undervalued. Page had been telling Peter Grant for a year that he had some strong ideas of what his next band would sound like and here it was in full glory. One peculiarity of the solo section is that it takes place over only seven occurrences of the main riff rather than the predictable eight as heard during the vocal verses. This choice was not duplicated on other versions of the song played by the band in concert as can be heard on BBC recordings and suggests Led Zeppelin was pandering to radio stations by keeping the total recording time of "Breakdown" to a more commercially accessible length. Regardless, the solo continues underneath Plant's return for the final chorus in which he concludes with an even more elongated and dramatic fall on the word *insane*. The song then drives to its conclusion as the main riff is repeated and slowly fades. During this egress, the song title is sung several times by the band in less-than-perfect harmonies while both Plant and Page offer up some final improvised interjections. Ending in less than two and a half minutes, "Breakdown" is the perfect example of a heavy-metal hit: the band builds the song upon a short, fast, and immediately recognizable riff; the guitar is raucous and distorted; the vocals emphasize pure energy over lyrical depth (or even comprehension); a guitar solo is the featured centerpiece; and the whole thing is over in well under three minutes.

"You Shook Me"

Based on a classic blues progression twelve measures in length with chords on which most aspiring rock musicians cut their teeth, "You Shook Me" is presented by Led Zeppelin in a slow, grinding tempo that is more difficult than a first listen will reveal. While an upbeat song like "Communication Breakdown" has its frenetic challenges, there are actually opportunities for musicians to disguise imperfections among the flurry of notes. In "You Shook Me" there is nowhere to hide. With so much space between the beats, the blemishes of an inexperienced or overconfident band will be quickly exposed. Led Zeppelin was ready for the task and even tested their mettle by facing comparison to another guitar-led rock band that recorded a version of the same Willie Dixon song five months earlier.

Jeff Beck, a member of the Yardbirds both before and during Page's tenure, created his rendition of "You Shook Me" with rising-star vocalist Rod Stewart, forever fueling speculation that Led Zeppelin "stole" the idea rather than work harder to separate themselves from the debut efforts of the Jeff Beck Group. Although this argument of claim jumping is bolstered by the fact that John Paul Jones plays organ on both versions, it diminishes when the recordings are played back to back. As phenomenal a guitarist as Beck was and has remained, his version of "You Shook Me" was riddled with problems. To begin with, the pianist Nicky Hopkins did just what he used to do on many rock recordings from the era: fill up sonic space with lots of embellishment. The same technique is heard on the original Dixon recording from Chess Records. But producer Mickie Most made the choice to mix the volume of both Hopkins's piano and Jones's organ much too loud, thus taking the emphasis away from a guitarist of Beck's stature. Secondly, Rod Stewart, one of the most successful rock vocalists ever to grab a microphone, was underserved by only singing two verses before giving way to instrumental solos and not to return. Lastly, the band plays the ending material so sloppily that it crosses the threshold of controlled looseness and approaches painfully awkward. So while it's true that Beck beat Led Zeppelin to the starting gate, his version of "You Shook Me" failed to exploit the potential of the song when the two are compared.

Page begins his "You Shook Me" with a searing, unaccompanied guitar line drenched in reverb and echo and is soon joined by drums, electric piano, and Plant's harmonica (the bass is provided by Jones on organ foot pedals). As the lyrics begin with "You know you shook me, you shook me all night long," we notice immediately that Page and Plant have taken the time to orchestrate their parts by performing the melody in unison. This guitar/vocal interplay would become a trademark of the band and the goal of many other rock bands to come. As the word *long* is held (a perfect example of "text painting" when the music delivery supports the lyric), the two musicians caress their way into a slow fall culminating in a brilliantly placed cymbal crash by Bonham as if a doomed cartoon character had finally hit bottom after dropping off a cliff. Heard first at thirty-three seconds into the track, Bonham repeats this punch line throughout the recording, although curiously, he often left the cymbal crash out when performing live, perhaps deciding that the joke had already been heard enough on the album.

In the classic blues form, the lyric of each verse is based on a brief opening phrase that allows room for improvisational fill before the same phrase is repeated. After the statement and restatement, a conclusion is offered that usually rhymes. "You Shook Me" follows this A-A-B form precisely, although Plant takes great liberties with his wide vocal range and rhythmic placement. Notice the increase in energy as he squeezes out the high notes in the conclusion of verse 1 on the word *baby*. Few male singers in the late 1960s were willing or able to belt out such pitches in full voice. Then, at the end of the second verse, he completely veers away from the expected response to "I have heard birds that sing" by wailing an improvised vocal line and tossing out a last-minute and nearly nondescript reference to a diamond ring. The confidence displayed in this abandonment of the pure lyric in favor of an emotional rumination is no small feat for a singer of only twenty years, but Plant pulls it off.

The third verse of "You Shook Me" features a tuneful and well-conceived organ solo from John Paul Jones. Although Jones spent most of his time playing bass for Led Zeppelin, his exceptional keyboard skills were often called for and on this solo he makes effective use of the

Leslie speaker that added to the iconic sound of the rock organ. The Leslie includes a rotating speaker with two horns at opposite ends from each other. As the device rotates, the sound coming through the horns is literally thrown forward from the speaker cabinet at intervals that simulate the vibrato of a vocalist. The speed of the rotation can also be adjusted to vary the effect and this is activated by a switch placed near the organ keyboard. The first three notes of the solo at 2:08 have no vibrato but you can hear how Jones flips the Leslie on for the fourth. He then returns to a "straight" tone at 2:15 for a few notes before spinning it up again at 2:19. By engaging and disengaging the Leslie speaker several times throughout a solo, Jones makes his instrument "sing" in a more stylized manner.

Considering the musical quality of Jones's organ playing and the guitar solo soon to come, Plant was given the difficult task of filling the entire fourth verse with a harmonica solo. Singers of the folk tradition are sometimes known for playing harmonica but there is a stereotype that their skill level is elementary at best. But in the tradition of blues singer/harmonica player Howling Wolf, Plant rises to the occasion here. Listen at 3:35 to how he interjects a vocalization between harmonica notes as if he is commenting on his own performance. The rest of his solo is choked full of idiomatic blues riffs that reveal Plant had listened to all the right records as a teenager. "You Shook Me" is one of only a few examples of Plant's harmonica playing in the Led Zeppelin catalog but if this track is any measure, the quality of his playing was not reason for the rarity.

On the fifth trip through the twelve-measure form of "You Shook Me," Page is finally let loose with a superior guitar feature. Although much of the *Led Zeppelin* album was recorded live, basically reproducing the set they had been performing at recent gigs, the solo to "You Shook Me" is an overdub that clearly demonstrates Page's ability to create a masterful improvisation when given time in the recording studio after his mates have left the building. Beginning at exactly four minutes into the track, Page opens up with a relaxed phrase of sustained notes that could just as well be the melody to an instrumental song rather than a solo "jam." At 4:10 he begins a second phrase that echoes the intent of the first but moves slightly higher up the scale. These rather conservative ideas deliver us to something we have yet to hear in the previous verses (or on recorded renditions from Beck or Dixon):

breaks, in which the band hits a chord together on the same beat and then stops playing, allowing space for the soloist to shine. Beginning at 4:19, the boys get out of the way as Page begins to crank up the pacing of his notes. We also notice the knockout punches coming from Bonham's ferocious drum fills that set up the next break. The band returns at 4:28 in what is almost a rhythmic train wreck as they seem to enter ahead of the expected beat, but they make a full recovery as Page presses on. Between 4:30 and 4:35, he returns to a simpler phrase of only a few notes but does so in a way that flirts between the echo effect and manually striking the same notes in repetition. After a few more seconds of strident note choices, Page closes out his composed solo with a classic blues idiom beginning at 4:47 telegraphing to all fans of the genre that his musical argument has reached its bruised, battered, and logical conclusion.

On the sixth and final verse of "You Shook Me," Plant returns with the same lyrics heard in the first verse, once again mimicked by Page's guitar and supported by Bonham's patient cymbal crash (although this time set up with a short but demonstrative drum fill). This book-end approach to playing a blues tune is not unusual but Led Zeppelin ends the song in a fashion so bombastic and ego-driven that upon the album's release, the question must have been asked, "Just who do these unproven youngsters think they are?"

At 5:38 in "You Shook Me" begins one of the most impressive dueling dialogues between a vocalist and guitarist to ever be recorded. With the rest of the musicians at a complete standstill, Plant takes the first shot with an impressively high singing of the word *babe* to which Page answers with the same note but hitting it twice. Then Plant mimics those two notes with wordless vocals, provoking Page to hit them again with a slight flourish. They repeat this volley several times before Page raises the stakes with a higher note at 5:47 that Plant is able to match but with apparent strain. Pushing the envelope even further, Page plays the same line but bends the strings to an even higher range. Unbelievably, Plant is able to reach into the vocal box stratosphere to match the notes perfectly. As if to acquiesce to Plant's daunting skill, Page drops down to sustain a note and waits for the singer to claim victory. With a gravel-torn but full voice, Plant shouts out a final "You shook me all night long" but hangs on "all" by twisting and turning the word for all it's worth, only relinquishing his grip and surrendering the last two words when he was utterly spent. To close the musical curtain on the scene, Page plays a brief unaccompanied riff before being joined by the band for the final chord drone and unsettled rumblings from Bonham's drums.

"How Many More Times"

Let's immediately clear the air that "How Many More Times" is not a jazz-based song. Led Zeppelin was not comprised of rogue jazzers looking to cash in on a hit record while sneaking in their fusionesque predilections with hopes of teaching their listeners what "good" music was through a side door. But, for the opening thirty-four seconds of "How Many More Times," it is reasonable to wonder just how close to the electric jazz stylings of Miles Davis's *Bitches Brew* Zeppelin is going to take us.

The track opens with Jones delivering a repetitive bass line lasting eight beats (two measures) that grooves along with a hint of bluesy notes and a walking feel used copiously throughout the history of jazz. This line is supported by Bonzo's crisp and swinging pattern on the ride cymbal with occasional accents on the toms or from striking the metal edge of the snare drum creating a solid but woody "click." This technique, referred to as a "side-stick," combined with the tom hits is a common rhythmic pattern often used by jazz drummers like Art Blakey. Even the entrance of Page's guitar at 0:08 does little to define the genre of what we are hearing. Instead of joining Jones on the main riff, Page fires off a chord with the agitated up-and-down strokes often used by string orchestra players, but does so with a relatively clean timbre that can be heard in many jazz or pop records of the same period. Only at 0:23 with the distant vocal wail of Plant do we become suspicious that something a bit more sinister is brewing. And finally, at 0:35, Bonzo trades the side-stick for a strong snare drum back-beat while Page rips off his mask of ambiguity, turns up the distortion, and we see the song for what it is—a riff-based rocker. Plant offers up confirmation of this unveiling upon his first verse when he asks twice with blues-drenched rhetorical wisdom, "How many times, treat me the way you wanna do?" Although the harmony does not move to the chords often heard in a blues progression, Plant's vocals follow the bluesy A-A-B pattern by repeating the opening statement and then answering with, "When I

give you all my love, please, please be true." Even though the song has
developed into a solid rocker, the influence of the blues is not far away.

Since the music under the opening verses is comprised only of the
riff heard since the first measures, the band provides a sonic border in
front of the second verse at 1:19 in the form of two sets of three rapid
chord hits. It isn't much of a deviation, but serves to communicate that
the musicians are paying attention to where they are and don't mind
telegraphing the information to the listener. The lyrics of the second
verse again follow the A-A-B pattern with the opening statement of "I
give you all I got to give; rings, pearls and all" resolved with "I got to get
you together baby; I'm sure you're gonna call." Throughout this verse
Bonham is heard thoroughly enjoying himself by playing several fills
and crashing away at the cymbals. By the 1980s this style of playing was
dropped in favor of nonsuperfluous, machine-perfect repetition but in
the late 1960s drummers like Keith Moon and Ginger Baker could still
mercilessly attack their instruments with impunity and in "How Many
More Times" Bonham takes full advantage of the opportunity.

Only after two minutes is there finally a clear departure from the
main riff as we hear the band playing a succession of sustained chords,
each lasting eight beats. The first new chord is slightly lower in pitch
before returning to the home key again. Meanwhile, Bonham continues
his fill-fest barrage, setting up the entrance of each chord. These two
chords are alternated for about one minute as Page patiently unfolds a
beautifully crafted solo consisting of two separate guitar parts overdubbed after the basic tracks were laid down. Listen to how the dueling
solos sometimes overlap and then depart as if Page is suggesting two
unique personalities that are both evading and pursuing each other. In
live performances, this section of the song was elongated into an epic
improvisational experience but for the studio version the band begins to
segue to the next section at 3:02. Bonham is the first to break ranks by
beginning what is called a "bolero" rhythm on his snare drum (listen for
the *dut da-da-da dut* pattern). As Jones joins with the drummer, Page's
two guitars begin speaking together as one voice in a melody that gradually builds in intensity. At 3:21 the two guitars break into harmony, thus
completing their transitional journey as competitors, then respectful
peers, and finally, harmonious partners. Underneath it all, the band
pounds away in note groupings of three (called "triplets") that seem in
peril of having no end until Jones takes the lead at 3:32 in a descending

bass line lasting eight beats. The bassist finally hits bottom and delivers the band to the next section of what is now revealed to be a considerably more sophisticated composition than the one-riff jam it might have been.

At 3:36 into "How Many More Times" it seems the song may have ended. The band arrives at the same note on the same beat and suddenly stops, leaving nothing but a hint of wafting reverb. If Zeppelin were primarily concerned with getting this song on the radio, then the length at this point was about right, but they had "Communication Breakdown" to keep programming directors happy and were obviously developing "How Many More Times" as a work of compositional depth. This was not a "single" intended to be a pop-music snack. Rather, this was a grand finale on a complete album meant to be savored as part of a multicourse dinner.

The silence is only left hanging for a moment before Zeppelin pounces on another chord and segues into another improvisational section, but this time led by the returning vocals of Plant. In what might be described in simplistic terms as a "hippie-music jam," Plant croons about lost loves and missed chances while the band improvises in an ethereal manner emphasized by Page's use of the violin bow on his guitar. Close your eyes at this point and you shouldn't have to try hard to imagine kaleidoscope effects and the scent of burning incense. Plant even throws in a little good-natured humor when he sings, "Whoops, oh Lord I did it again. Now I've got ten children of my own. I've got another child on the way; that makes eleven. But I'm in constant heaven." Soon, the band ramps up the energy with the returning triplet feel at 5:15 but this time stretches it out even longer. Beginning to sound as if they might teeter over a mountain any moment, Jones once again comes to the rescue at 5:27 with a more pronounced version of the descending figure he played earlier, saving the day and propelling them forward to yet one more section of the song.

At 5:31, Page, Jones, and Bonham come to a smashing hit together and then quickly mute their instruments to leave room for Plant's searing vocal interjections. Hit: "Oh, Rosie." Hit: "Oh girl." Hit: "Steal away now." Hit: "Steal away." And so forth. Bonham kicks into a serious groove at 5:50 as Plant makes the autobiographical reference that "Little Robert Anthony wants to come and play." Letting Bonzo and Plant carry most of the load for a while, Page and Jones introduce a new riff at

6:08 that would be considered worthy of a song all on its own. It was almost arrogant of the boys to toss out a riff this good near the end of a song rather than saving it for another day.

Played with a sense of menace, Zeppelin took this riff into what was now the sixth section of "How Many More Times." Fans of Albert King will quickly recognize Plant's lyrics as taken from "The Hunter" released in 1967 on King's *Born Under a Bad Sign* album. "The Hunter" was quickly covered by other groups like Free, Canned Heat, and Blue Cheer. So it isn't surprising Plant picked up a piece of the lyric for himself: "They call me the hunter; that's my name. They call me the hunter; that's how I got my fame." Then, as Page and Jones move to chords typical at the end of a blues progression, Plant sings, "Ain't no need to hide, ain't no need to run, 'cause I got you in the sights of my gun." But this is where things get dangerously more interesting.

Zeppelin's brief encounter with the blues is a cool deviation but what they need at this point is, like must be found in any worthy epic rocker, a way to get back to their original riff. The problem is that they have veered far away from the opening groove and even sped up the tempo somewhat, making a smooth return difficult. The solution was found in the two old mates Plant and Bonham. As Plant sings, "cause I got you," Page and Jones drop out and leave Bonham to do the work of slowing the tempo down by steady hits on his hi-hat. With only Bonham's subtle time keeping for accompaniment, Plant sets a new limit for what rock singers are capable of. Using the word *gun* as a launching pad at 6:57, Plant sweeps upward from his chest voice into a powerful head-voice scream that has left vocalists shaking their heads in disbelief for decades. While Plant holds the shockingly high note, Bonham cracks his snare drum as a cue for Page and Jones to jump in on the opening riff that hasn't been heard for several minutes but conjures visions of warriors returning victoriously from the field of battle.

Now in full force and driving "How Many More Times" toward its finality (albeit at a slightly faster tempo than the one set at the beginning), Plant calls out at 7:12, "How many more times, barrel house all night long?" At 8:03 the band plays a more relaxed version of triplet hits as Plant pleads, "Why won't you please come home?" Repeating this figure three more times, Bonham grinds the tempo down before the now-idiomatic hard-rock ending in which all the players essentially pile on the last chord and conclude with one final unison hit.

And at that moment, Led Zeppelin's first album comes to a close. Listening to it on the media of the day in 1969, the needle of the turntable lifts off the center wax of the record and returns to the cradle while the newly won Led Zeppelin fan sits dumbfounded knowing rock music will never be the same.

2

RAMBLING ON

Zeppelin was a band on the run in 1969. They recorded their second album, *Led Zeppelin II*, at various studios as they toured America in support of their freshman effort, which had proven wildly successful. Their follow-up release did not stray far from the template of *Led Zeppelin* except they now took the time to write more of their own material and rely less on pre-existing blues numbers or Page's leftovers from the Yardbirds. This collection of recordings fully announced Led Zeppelin as the lords of riff rock and roll. Rather than concern themselves with the verse-chorus form of radio-friendly pop records, Page and Jones preferred to write songs based primarily on brief, repetitive, and powerful riffs that listeners found irresistible and aspiring guitarists could mimic. Lyrics, in turn, were freed from the limitations imposed by strict verse-chorus structures and Plant found creative ways to anchor his songs on a short hook or catch phrase. This compositional technique would forever define not only Led Zeppelin, but also the entire genre of riff-based rock that they came to dominate.

A sales pitch for the first track on *Led Zeppelin II* might just as well have been, "If you like 'Communication Breakdown,' you'll love 'Whole Lotta Love!'" The two songs are in the same guitar-friendly key of E, the tempo is similar, the vocals enter on the same gravel-laden high note (B natural), and Page leads the way with fiery introductions of unaccompanied guitar riffs. And yet, each song is completely unique and would never be confused for the other. Page and company developed an ability early on to take songs that on paper should sound all too

familiar and make them entirely unique. As you listen through the
Zeppelin canon, there are no occasions where you will be inclined to
say, "That sounds just like the bit from their earlier album." A knowl-
edgeable Zeppelin fan will cite how "Riverside Blues" is a recasting of
the lyrics to "Lemon Song," but "Riverside" was only released on a
boxed set years after the band's demise. When it comes to the material
spread across their nine studio albums, Zeppelin had the exceptional
ability to make the same old stuff sound like a pretty young thing. For a
closer look at "Whole Lotta Love," see below.

   "What Is and What Should Never Be" is the second song on *Led
Zeppelin II* and the opening moments couldn't offer a more stark
contrast to "Whole Lotta Love." Plant gives his vocals a loving touch.
Bonham floats on his cymbals. Jones dances melodically. And Page
strums a campfire sing-along. A mom and dad listening outside their
teenager's room in 1969 might even look at each other and whisper,
"Those Zeppelin lads can't be all bad." Of course, it's all a ruse to be
blown asunder but it demonstrates how the band knew that being loud
sounds better if preceded by soft. Too many other bands have never
understood that basic law of acoustics. For a closer look at "What Is and
What Should Never Be," see below.

   "The Lemon Song" is not only the third song on *Led Zeppelin II*, but
also the third song in a row in the key of E. Normally, if there are a few
songs in the same key on one album there is an attempt to spread them
out so that the ear hears more tonal variation between songs. That really
isn't an option of *Led Zeppelin II* because five of the nine songs are all
centered around E. This harmonic faux pas is surpassed on their fourth
album where the key of A graces each of the first five tracks. Their
proclivity to reuse favorite keys was all the more reason for the band to
find more eloquent ways to distinguish their songs from each other.
"The Lemon Song" stands above the crowd with an exceptionally memorable climbing riff and a multisectioned compositional form. It is a
recording like this that gives the term *hard rock* a place to call home.
For a closer look at "The Lemon Song," see below.

   Plant took more of a complete role as lyricist during *Led Zeppelin II*
and that is decidedly evident on "Thank You." This delicate number is
dedicated to Plant's wife (at the time) and opens with the sincerely
romantic, "If the sun refused to shine, I would still be loving you."
Under such sentiment we hear the dulcet church organ from Jones and

the folksong embrace of Page on his twelve-string guitar. "Thank You" is a lovely and most unexpected summer rain in the midst of heavy thunder. And the acoustic guitar solo from Page is a gem. Too bad he felt obliged to sing backup harmonies.

"Heartbreaker" is yet another perfect guitar riff. It's repetitive, not too long, not too short, not too fast, not too slow, and—most important-ly—easy for young guitarists to play when trying to impress others in the neighborhood music store. This one has something for the bass players too. The tone Jones uses is monstrous and it's a shame he didn't duplicate it more often. Even though the main riff is derived from notes of what guitarists know as the "blues scale," Jones and Page don't take the easy way out and write a song using the well-traveled blues progression. Instead, they choose the unique path of transposing the main riff upward several times during the verse. With each successive phrase from Plant we step a little higher and increase the forward energy of the song. Plant is so good at writing melodies that have little to do with the guitar riff of the moment, but on "Heartbreaker" he takes the Ozzy Osbourne approach from Black Sabbath's "Ironman" and simply shadows the riff of Page and Jones. But no one notices the lyrics much on this one anyway. It's all about the solo guitar break at 2:03. Page's unaccompanied "cadenza" doesn't shine brightly after several decades. The playing is sloppy and not technically demanding. But at the time of release it was bold and inspiring to young boys (Slash) and girls (Nancy Wilson), who began to think of "guitar hero" as a pretty cool idea.

"Living Loving Maid" is a rare weak link in the chain of Zeppelin's catalog. The song has a modicum of late 1960s charm but is not up to the band's usual level of competence. They needed one more song for the album and this one slipped through. Zeppelin had been performing "We're Gonna Groove" in concert around this time and it's too bad they didn't get it recorded in time for the release of *Led Zeppelin II*. But on a positive note, perhaps the concept of alternating between the vocals and a riff as heard in "Living Loving Maid" opened the path to the Zeppelin powerhouse "Black Dog," which came later.

"Ramble On" contains some of the most notable bass playing Jones ever contributed to a Led Zeppelin record. In fact, it's some of the most notable bass playing on *any* rock record. Not because of speed or fin-ger-tapping virtuosic playing. It's just Jones playing with a beautiful sense of melody and rhythmic interest that is not usually accommodated by the demands or expectations of rock music. Bassists spend most of their time doubling the guitar riff or pounding out notes that don't stray far from the root of the chord. But in the case of "Ramble On," Jones does neither and the result is profound. Plant has written a great lyric (the Gollum reference has grown quaint over the decades) and the guitar riff during the chorus is among Page's best.

"Moby Dick" is hopelessly lost in the late 1960s. The rock-hard riff is drenched in timelessness by the blues-bending syncopation of Page and Jones but then it gives way to that most dated of epic elements—the drum solo. Grand Funk Railroad did it in "T. N. U. C." Iron Butterfly had "In-A-Gadda-Da-Vida." Ginger Baker took his turn in "Toad" from Cream. Even the Beatles gave Ringo his space on "The End." If you are too young to have experienced it at the time, all rock bands of the era featured lengthy drum solos during their concerts and these percussive explorations sometimes made their way on to a studio album. "Moby Dick" was the medium through which John "Bonzo" Bonham thrilled audiences, especially when he tossed his sticks and played with nothing but his hands. The sense of Bonham's visual intensity is neutered when captured in the studio rather than a concert hall but within the context of "drum-solo songs," it doesn't get any better.

The final track on *Led Zeppelin II* is "Bring It on Home" including material originally written by Willie Dixon and recorded by Sonny Boy Williamson in 1963. The blistering riff and soulful singing in the middle is all Zeppelin but as a tribute to their respect for Williamson, an intro-duction and ending were added that essentially imitated the previous recording. Plant even mimics with great accuracy the harmonica playing and animated vocal vibrato. Such "tributes" were typical of rock bands throughout the late 1960s but by the 1970s most of the honorees rightly responded with lawsuits for copyright infringement. In the case of "Bring It on Home," it's a highlight in the Zeppelin catalog and in subsequent releases Dixon is rightfully given a songwriting credit.

A CLOSER LOOK

"Whole Lotta Love"

The main riff to "Whole Lotta Love" is not complicated. It includes only three different pitches with the main "key" (E in this case) getting most of the attention. But the way those notes are laid out on the guitar and bass make all the difference to how they sound. As guitarists can confirm, playing rock in the key of E just feels good. There is a depth and power that comes from the lower strings that can't be found in other keys. Page knew this all too well when he created a riff for the ages by keeping it simple and giving it a rhythm that emulates a train moving at only a modest pace but with the weight and horsepower to blast through any barrier. Lasting about five and a half minutes, "Whole Lotta Love" is a rather simple song from a compositional viewpoint. There's not much going on other than *the* riff. But the recording is timeless nonetheless due to the supreme performance of the Led Zeppelin members and the wizardly production of Page as he took a single riff and manifested a hard-rock masterpiece.

"Whole Lotta Love" opens with a brief laugh from Plant quickly interrupted by Page's centerpiece riff using a fully overdriven guitar timbre. Jones joins in for the second pass and then the two of them accompany the vocals with no drums. The lyric, beginning with "You need coolin', baby I'm not foolin'," would eventually prove troublesome because Plant lifted it from a Muddy Waters recording called "You Need Loving" (also written by Willie Dixon) released in 1962. In later years there were court cases and settlements but there in 1969, Plant was hurriedly writing songs in the midst of touring and took the easy way out when he needed a lyric. In the June 1990 issue of *Musician*, Plant described the situation:

> Page's riff was Page's riff. It was there before anything else. I just thought, "Well, what am I going to sing?" That was it, a nick; now happily paid for. At the time, there was a lot of conversation about what to do. It was decided that it was so far away in time and influence that . . . well, you only get caught when you're successful. That's the game.

Waiting patiently for thirty-three seconds, Bonham finally breaks into the recording with a drum fill that sets up his steady rock groove played under the next round of vocals. As is the style of many blues songs, there is no change in the harmony/chords between the verse and chorus in "Whole Lotta Love." Instead, the main riff simply soldiers on as Plant sings the hook "Wanna whole lotta love" four times with Page playing an overdubbed, downward-sliding guitar effect between each.

The second verse kicks off at 0:47 with words not present in the Waters version, "You've been yearnin'. Baby, I've been learnin'. All them good times baby, baby I've been discernin'." The succeeding chorus is nearly identical to the first but on the last "Wanna whole lotta love" the band moves directly into a drawn-out psychedelic jam. Beginning at 1:18, this section is a combination of Bonham's steady time keeping on the hi-hat and the group efforts of Page, Plant, and audio engineer Eddie Kramer. Page creates a montage of aural effects by the use of an electric instrument called the Theremin. Listen at 1:45 to the swirling volume increase as Page manipulates the Theremin with echo. The result is quite evocative when heard in stereo as the splashes of sound chase from the left to right speakers.

Then Plant returns at 2:03 with a series of what can be considered pre-, mid-, and post-orgasmic moaning. These lurid interjections were part of the reason radio stations shied away from playing the track and some disc jockeys went as far as to create their own abbreviated versions that cut the potentially offensive (and time-consuming) portion. In order to appease, Led Zeppelin released their own abbreviated version with a similar edit but it was never intended for commercial sale and originally made available only to radio stations. At 2:47, Plant shouts out a primal "LOOOOOVE" that jumps out of the speakers with its single-minded and desperate sincerity. A few seconds later he repeats his mating call but is this time matched by a churning Theremin that seems to be driving the aforementioned train right off the rails. It is Bonham that comes to the rescue at 3:02 by imitating a machine gun on his snare drum and herding the players back from their acid-fueled departure.

A less adventurous band would have simply returned to the main riff at this point but Page had other plans. The band comes out of Bonham's drum fill with two ferocious hits at 3:05, the first on a downbeat and the second on an upbeat creating a rhythmic syncopation with a hint of mayhem. Zeppelin continues this duo of hits five more times and between each, Page strings together a series of unaccompanied solo jewels. Playing a total of six groups of hits was an unusual choice since most pop and rock songs are comprised of sections divided by four. Recall that Zeppelin made a similarly odd choice by having a guitar solo on "Communication Breakdown" last only seven units. When "Whole Lotta Love" was performed live, the band seemed to consider this section flexible, playing anywhere from six to as many as ten groupings before moving on. But for the purposes of the record, four was not enough and eight might have been indulgent, so six it was.

"You been coolin'; baby I've been droolin'" is the lyric at 3:20 when Page's guitar solo concludes and he returns finally to the A-section riff with the support of Jones on bass. Cultivating his rock-god persona, Plant continues with the lyric "I'm gonna give you every inch of my love" before the band reaches the third chorus. That was only the beginning of Plant's cheekiness when the band stops at 3:58 and he steps up for a vocal-only break with the words "Way down inside, woman, you need it." Of course, the insinuation is that the woman in his song needs sexual gratification that only Plant can supply, but with a bit of a wink to proper decorum he adds the word *love* as if that was all he meant. You'll notice in this section that there is a quieter version of Plant's vocals that actually precedes the full-volume voice. This was more studio trickery performed after the fact by Page and Kramer using an echo effect and shifting its location. This has the odd result of letting you hear the lyric slightly earlier than you are expecting, but it does not diminish the quality of Plant's main delivery. Page long ago claimed this "reverse echo" effect as his own invention.

Beginning at 4:22, Plant ends his a cappella section by singing the word *love* at an incredibly high note and slowly sliding downward through his impressive vocal range. This was the exact opposite musical response to his upward sweep on the word *gun* in "How Many More Times" from Zeppelin's first album. This type of gymnastic vocalization had not been an expected part of a rock singer's toolbox before Plant, but has been ever since. His youthful voice seemed unlimited by normal constraints and he was pleased to often demonstrate such abilities.

As captivating as this vocal slide is, Bonham brings us back to the task at hand, which is ending the song. His evenly paced fill on the snare drum brings the band in at 4:28 for one last bout with the main riff leading to a full minute of jamming while Plant improvises. With lyrics like "I wanna be your backdoor man" Plant continues his double entendre blues references borrowed from a Howlin' Wolf recording.

Notice also at this point how Page and Jones tinker with the riff in two ways. Beginning at 4:28, they now play the pick-up notes that set up the riff every four beats instead of the previous eight. This has the subtle yet noticeable effect of increasing the momentum of the music. To return one more time to the train analogy, the locomotive appears to have picked up speed even though the engine is turning at the same revolutions per minute. The second tweak is Page playing an over-dubbed guitar part with a slightly higher note on every second playing of these pick up notes. Listen closely at 5:02, 5:07, or 5:12 for examples. This is an early example of Page building up multiple guitar lines in an orchestral manner. Meanwhile, Bonham is throwing out a succession of drum fills as Plant continues his pseudo-sexual wailing until the overall volume begins to noticeably fade around 5:20. Zeppelin would create a definitive ending of "Whole Lotta Love" for live performance but on the record they allowed the tune to simply roll on down the tracks in a way that suggests it never really ends. The party just rolls on to the next city, where respectable folks would be wise to shutter the windows and hide their daughters.

"What Is and What Should Never Be"

Rock bass players don't get much respect compared to the rest of a band. Vocalists have the dominating stage presence. Guitarists have the mystique and featured solos. And drummers grab the spotlight with flailing appendages. But bassists? Don't they just hover off to the side playing one note at a time? Jimmy Page himself is partly responsible for tarnishing the perception of how little experience a bass player needs to be in a rock band. He was so anxious to join the Yardbirds as a means to get out of the studio session grind that he accepted the only position open—that of bassist—even though he had never played the instrument. Such actions only fueled the reputation that bass players were really just frustrated guitarists who had drawn the short straw when school mates chose the instruments each would play in their new band. But there were a few bassists who rose above low expectations the public (and even other musicians) placed on the instrument. John Entwistle of the Who, Mel Schacher of Grand Funk Railroad, and Geddy Lee of Rush are a few. And without reservation add to that list Led Zeppelin's own John Paul Jones, or "Jonesy" as the band members called him. Although he could play the traditional rock-bass figure in which the low note of each chord is repetitively hammered on, Jones was also well schooled in the James Jamerson style (Jamerson was the primary bassist for Motown Records during the 1960s and early 1970s) that allowed for a more active, melodic, and rhythmically varied role. It was on "What Is and What Should Never Be" that Jones demonstrated this influence and began to assert himself as an intrinsic element of the emerging Zeppelin sound.

As Plant opens "What Is and What Will Never Be" with the unaccompanied lyric "And if I say to you tomorrow," the rest of the band enters in a deliberately laid back manner. Bonham lightly plays a subdued pulse on the cymbal. Page draws on his knowledge of jazz by delicately playing rich harmonies called ninth or thirteenth chords mimicking a one-strum-per-beat rhythm Freddie Green often used with the Count Basie orchestra. But listen to the bass in the opening phrases and you'll notice Jones is providing the only melodically interesting music during the first twenty-five seconds. This exemplifies the subtle but masterful bass lines Jones often contributed to Zeppelin recordings. They might slip by largely unnoticed during a first listen, but remove them and the foundation of the entire song collapses from boredom.

With a quick snare-drum fill, the band transitions from the A section (verse) to the B section (chorus) of the tune, where Page kicks up his overdriven guitar tone over a Bonham drum beat flush with energy. But once again, it is the bass riff of Jones that actively propels the groove forward. Imagine how less interesting the music would be without this part, and yet it is the voice and guitar that most likely garner the attention of the uninformed rocker.

While Plant's voice is modified by a widening effect in the A section called a "chorus" (not to be confused with a section of a song with the same name), during the B section he thickens the vocal sound by using the double-tracking technique heard on Zeppelin's first album. The separate voices might be hard to detect at first but unapologetically reveal themselves at 0:38 when you can hear Plant sing both a primary melody and an overdubbed secondary harmony on the lyric "and you will be mine by taking our time." Considering that harmony vocals were used sparingly in the Zeppelin catalog, shifting from one voice to two at this lyrical moment is no coincidence. By singing in two-part harmony, Plant aurally fulfills the implication of the lyric. As a direct means to wrap up the energetic chorus and return to the verse's mellow flavor, Plant simply sings a sustained harmony with the syllable "ooh" while the band takes their collective foot off the gas pedal and gently rolls to a stop at 0:50. This has the pleasant and unusual (in a rock or pop song) effect of temporarily suspending the tempo. We are asked to reflect a moment on what we've just heard, and only when Plant is good and ready to intone the next verse are we allowed to proceed.

With the words "And if you say to me tomorrow," Plant leads the band into the second A section at 0:57, which is performed in identical fashion to the first. Jones again leads the relaxed frivolity while Plant drops the title into the song when singing "And what's to stop us pretty baby, but what is and what should never be." Plant makes ample use of the word *baby* on Zeppelin's first few albums, often in a high register and calling out for attention, but here he adds an extra couple notes to the second syllable and playfully drops downward in pitch, thus fulfilling the promise in the immediately preceding lyric, "Oh what fun it all would be."

The band once again stalls the tempo at the end of the second B section but instead of being revived by more vocals, this time Page steps into the spotlight. At 1:47 he uses a finger slide to play a solo so singable it could just as well have served as Plant's vocal melody. This was the craftsman at work. We can hear many solos from Page in which he seems to primarily "jam" ("Communication Breakdown," "Good Times, Bad Times," and later, "Stairway to Heaven"), but in "What Is and What Should Never Be" Page creates a solo from the perspective of a patient composer. He starts with a new melody and slowly develops it in methodical and interesting ways. Notice how he quickly repeats the initial melodic statement at 1:53 but adds variety by adding a second guitar playing in harmony. Then at 1:59 he reverts back to the single guitar but adds novelty by sending the signal back and forth across the stereo field (headphones or ear buds will help you appreciate the subtlety). At 2:12 Bonham ratchets up the intensity with a few hits on his snare and although Page responds with a louder tone, he still plays a rather conservative figure in which he repeatedly slides into the same note. Only at 2:23 does the guitarist finally shift to a higher note while not abandoning the same "sliding into home" effect. Composers refer to this technique of tying one melodic phrase into the next as "unity" (the opposite being "variety") and Page was quite comfortable with the concept. His solo ends at 2:40 with a long, downward slide that hands the attention back to the returning lyrics of Plant (with Jones still keeping busy on the bass).

After another vocal verse and chorus, the listener is left to wonder what compositional tactics have yet to be exploited by Zeppelin as they come to a third respite at 3:30. Another verse with lyrics? Perhaps another verse featuring the guitar? Hardly. Instead, the band tosses out a new riff-based section that any other band would relish as the main foundation of a song. But Zeppelin had enough confidence in their future creative output that hoarding golden riffs for later albums never occurred to them. Page is the first to announce the new material as the series of two-chord hits dance back and forth across the stereo spectrum. Bonham contributes a bombastic crash on a gong at 3:37, Jones drops in a complementary bass line at 3:43, and the sonic pyramid is complete with both Bonham and Plant joining in earnest at 3:50. With lyrics like "Everybody I know seems to know me well but does anybody know I'm gonna move like hell" delivered with a full-throttled, bluesy tone, this final section of "What Is and What Should Never Be" rocks mightily. Similar to "Whole Lotta Love," we hear a fade begin around 4:30 with Plant's trademark, high-note repetition of the word *baby* and are left wishing one thing—that the boys in the band wouldn't leave so soon.

"Lemon Song"

The third track on *Led Zeppelin II* is a mash-up of several blues songs Zeppelin had been performing during their first tours and is a powerful example of how they converted traditional blues into something original for a new generation. Similar to much of the material on their first album, Zeppelin recorded the "Lemon Song" live in the studio with very little tinkering in post production. Using a small recording space at Mystic Studios in Hollywood, California, the band captured a realistic representation of what it was like to hear Led Zeppelin at a concert in 1969.

The "Lemon Song" opens up with yet another gong blast from Bonham as Page introduces a simple but potent riff borrowed heavily from "Killing Floor" by Howlin' Wolf (his real name was Chester Burnett). The tempo here is on the slow side, much slower than Wolf's original version, and suggests the rough grind of slowly churning wheels. Page's guitar is panned hard to one side of the stereo field so it is easy to differentiate it from Jones's bass panned in the opposite direction. Jones and Bonham (with the drums set dead center in the stereo mix) enter at 0:12 and the groove is underway.

Riffs in old blues-based songs are often considered fair game among songwriters and Zeppelin would likely have not been held accountable if they had only used Wolf's music as a background to new lyrics. But the band had been performing "Killing Floor" since their earliest concerts and even though the song had morphed into something more original through their nightly extended jams, Plant made no attempts to create a new lyric for the opening verses of "Lemon Song." Fans of Howlin' Wolf will immediately recognize Plant's borrowed opening line of "I should have quit you, long time ago" and the response "I wouldn't be here my children, down on this killin' floor." For anyone uncertain, the "killing floor" is a blues metaphor for a sad and lonely place to be. The original release of *Led Zeppelin II* did not credit Wolf as a songwriter even though the music and lyric were clear lifts so it was no surprise when Wolf's music publisher sued in 1972. The details of the settlement are not in the public record but Wolf is said to have received a check for over $45,000 soon after the case was dropped and he is cited as a songwriter in later releases of the album.

Returning to the recording, Plant singing "I wouldn't be here my children" is a perfect example of Zeppelin delivering on a technique that might be called "loosely tight." At 0:42, Page, Jones, and Bonham suddenly veer from their individual roles to join forces by playing a short phrase that lifts into the last four measures of the blues progression. You'll notice that even though they are playing together, there is a slight tilt to the unity, as if they were delightfully caught off guard by their own synchronicity. Thus, they are musically tight, but still loose. Few other rock bands have ever achieved a similar cohesiveness even if Zeppelin members were involved. Years later, when Page performed a full Zeppelin set with the Black Crowes, their version of "Lemon Song" is a convincing rendition but the same musical phrase (heard at 0:51 on their *Live at the Greek* album) is far more studied and mathematically precise. It was Zeppelin that seemed to have mastered the ability to make imperfection indispensable to the rhythmic groove. This is not unlike many great ensembles from rock or jazz. Arrangements from the Duke Ellington or Count Basie catalog can be performed by other groups, but the end result just doesn't swing with the same barely controlled edginess of the originals.

The first and second verses of "Lemon Song" are delineated with another joining of the minds among the band. As soon as Plant delivers his verse 1 summation, Jones and Page meld together on a solo line that sounds improvised but must have been worked out ahead of time. To provide this figure at 0:51 even more emphasis, Page overdubs a second guitar playing the same riff but pans it to the opposite side of the stereo mix so that it stands distinct from his original track. This brief addition of another guitar tips off the listener that there is likely more to be heard from Page in the coming minutes.

The next verse, starting at 0:55, begins with Plant singing "I should have listened baby to my second mind" and is also taken from Wolf's "Killing Floor." It's tempting to correlate Plant's "second mind" with the addition of Page's second guitar. At 1:07 is a brief but noticeable "mistake" played by Page. At this point in the progression/riff, the first note in that measure should have moved to the new chord but Page plays the first note from the earlier chord instead. The two notes aren't dissonant and would likely pass unnoticed by the casual listener, but even so, most producers/musicians would insist on fixing the blemish in order to be consistent with how Page played all the other verses. But Zeppelin was short on studio time while traveling across America in 1969 and their leaving the track as it was serves as a reminder that classic recordings are not necessarily hindered by the occasional mis-step when the overall vibe is right.

The second verse ends with the same delineating solo line as the first but is chopped short for a new excursion. At 1:28 the band shifts gears and begins a lengthy instrumental section that finds its inspiration in the Wolf recording but with one major modification—the tempo is completely different and unexpected. When analyzed by a metronome, the pulse of the opening verses of "Lemon Song" moves along at about 88 beats per minute (bpm). It isn't atypical at all in pop music for a song to transition to a "double time" feel that in this case would register at 176 bpm or even "half time" (44 bpm) but Zeppelin does something danger-ously unusual by increasing the pulse to an unrelated 145 bpm (for comparison, Wolf's version is 110 bpm). This kind of seemingly random tempo change just wasn't done in the rock music of 1969, but Zeppelin had the audacity to ignore the norm. Successfully maneuvering back and forth between the two tempos (more than once as we shall hear) is a testament to their musicianship, sense of adventure, and willingness to document in the studio what might have happened as an unplanned deviation one night during a concert.

Zeppelin propels their way through this instrumental section with Page leading the attack while Jones keeps pace and Bonham cracks away at the snare drum on every pulse. We now hear the second guitar take over as the dominant sound in the mix and this continues into the next chorus of the chord progression when Page begins a more tradi-tional lead-guitar work at 1:47. Lasting two trips through the twelve-bar progression, this solo has a strongly improvised quality but was well crafted by Page. His solo playing on "Lemon Song" is rife with iconic licks that reveal nods of acknowledgment to guitarists Page was well aware of such as Buddy Guy, Albert King, and Hubert Sumlin (Howlin' Wolf's guitarist for many years).

At 2:24 the band (especially Jones and Bonham) proves their worth by grabbing the tempo by the throat and dragging it down to the origi-nal pace—not an easy task. This is the aural equivalent to launching a satellite probe into orbit where just being a few clicks too far left or right leads to catastrophe. The arrival point must simply be dead on target. To announce this feat, Plant returns with a raspy, full-voiced wail that lasts an eyebrow-raising nine seconds. He had remained patient for the duration of Page's solo exploits and now charges forth like an unfed and finally uncaged animal.

The band continues through this verse in a mostly improvisational style with no set lyrics as they bide their time toward the next feature. Plant gives us a hint of what's to come by calling out at 2:55 to "take it down a little bit." The group responds to his plea and for the next few minutes Jones treats us to some of the best blues-centered bass playing of the era. Adding only a few colorful interjections, Page fades into the background while Plant improvises some blues lyrics that at times are largely indecipherable. But focus on the bass and drums and you will hear the very definition of the difficult-to-define "groove." Close your eyes and feel your body start to rhythmically move to the intricate but alluring interplay of Jones and Bonham. The two captured on tape a defining moment of their ability to listen and lock into each other's playing and even predict what the other was about to do.

As this tour de drum and bass continues, at 4:03 Plant makes still another lyrical reference to outside material when he sings, "Squeeze me baby 'till the juice runs down my leg," with the even cheekier response of "The way you squeeze my lemon I'm gonna fall right out of bed." This was a line from Robert Johnsons "Traveling Riverside Blues" recorded in 1937 and Zeppelin was well aware of the song, even recording their own cover version in June of 1969 (although not released until decades later). From this point on, references to lemons became a running joke for the band, with fans throwing them onstage and journalists working them into headlines. Plant even held a lemon in his hands in 1983 during a video for his solo-album song "In the Mood."

After another round of solo craftwork by Page, he and Plant present more of their trademark "call and response" cultivated from hours of onstage jamming. Beginning at 5:06 you can hear the two musically imitate and chase one another so that it's hard to be sure who is the caller and who is the responder. At 5:17, Plant once again shows us how the word *baby* was his plaything that could be used to present all forms of emotion.

This guitar/voice discourse finally winds down when the band revs up for one last run at the faster section heard earlier. At 5:37, Page breaks once again into the Hubert Sumlin guitar reference but with one more trick up his sleeve. He now adds a third guitar placed in the center of the stereo spectrum, adding even more energy to what is the band's finale to the song. Page pulls the band into one more twelve-measure progression with a last-gasp solo while Jones continues his brutal bass work and Bonham practically cracks away at his snare drum until coming to a crashing and immediate halt where Plant summarizes the entire song with "I'm gonna leave my children down on this killing floor." An echo of the band's last notes hangs briefly in the air before their grip is released.

3

SEX AND VIKINGS

Although *Led Zeppelin III*, released in 1970, contains many of the heavy metal and pseudo-sexual signatures expected of the band, critics panned the album—and badly, too—accusing Zeppelin of going soft. Page and Plant had written many of the songs while sequestered at a country cottage called Bron-Yr-Aur and the isolation on the moors did indeed bring out their folk influences with songs like "Gallows Pole," "That's the Way," and "Friends." The band even offered up a pop song with the chorus-driven "Tangerine." But to satisfy their ardent male-youth fan base, "Immigrant Song" powered ahead with one of the most iconic riff-rhythms ever recorded by a rock band. With lyrics referencing Valhalla and "tales of gore," Zeppelin only increased their growing reputation as rock music's "hammer of the gods" while actually broadening the band's appeal with the inclusion of acoustic material. They had their metal and would eat the critics too.

In 1978, Led Zeppelin's "Immigrant Song" jumped from being a cultish favorite on outlier FM radio right into our mainstream living rooms. On televisions everywhere tuned into the "Gong Show," Chuck Barris introduced the "Band from Nowhere" who came out in seven-foot alien costumes and performed a lip-sync/air-guitar version of "Immigrant Song." Zeppelin fans freaked out across America. Somehow the music of their beloved quartet had slipped through the "good taste" filters of mainstream television and represented "Immigrant Song" as worthy of artistic satire. The performers not only escaped the skit-ending gong, but also were awarded top scores by all three judges. It may be hard to fathom today when the antics of rock stars are mundane front-page fodder, but in the 1970s such coverage was simply not done. "If we ignore it, maybe they'll go away" was the mantra of media content programmers who considered Captain and Tennille's "Do That to Me One More Time" as racy as they dare go. But on one fateful night, somebody somewhere let down their guard and the mighty Zeppelin was at the tip of the spear. Many Zeppelin fans will admit they had never heard the band before that fateful night on the Gong Show and felt an irresistible pull toward the pounding rhythm and siren call of "Immigrant Song."

On the classic Zeppelin bootleg album, *Live on Blueberry Hill* (recorded at the Los Angeles Forum on September 4, 1970), Plant takes a moment to describe the hideaway that served as their songwriting retreat:

> This is a name of the little cottage in the mountains of Snowdonia in Wales, and "Bron-Yr-Aur" is the Welsh equivalent of the phrase "Golden Breast." This is so because of its position every morning as the sun rises and it's a really remarkable place. And so after staying there for a while and deciding it was time to leave for various reasons, we couldn't really just leave it and forget about it.

"Friends," is another Bron-Yr-Aur composition from Plant-Page and the second track on *Led Zeppelin III*. The guitarist uses an alternate tuning of his guitar strings that provides a more open sound and Plant matches his lyrics wonderfully to the mood of the music. "Friends" marks the first use of orchestral strings on a Zeppelin recording and is the result of Jones's skill as an arranger. In a peculiar act of oversight and/or disrespect, Jones's considerable contribution to the song is left uncredited. Nonetheless, Zeppelin leads us to think their third album is a hard-rock assault with "Immigrant Song" but by following up with "Friends," we aren't sure what to expect next.

Once upon a time in the 1970s, rock bands like Zeppelin focused on making complete albums of music in which the songs were unified by subject, sound, personnel, or perhaps just a general vibe of intention. This was a paradigm shift from the previous emphasis on 45 rpm singles and predated the much later transition to individual songs sold as digital downloads (of which Zeppelin was one of the last holdouts). Bands and their producers would look for ways to connect the songs across an album and in the case of *Led Zeppelin III*, a simple example of bridge material is heard between the second and third tracks.

Listen to the beginning of "Celebration Day" and you hear a growling Moog synthesizer that soon fades into the background and has no bearing on the rest of the song. But if you were listening to the album in 1970 you wouldn't have thought it was odd in any way because the keyboard effect is begun during the end of the previous "Friends" recording and carries over into "Celebration Day," thus providing connective tissue and tethering the listening experience between the two otherwise disparate songs. This big-picture production treatment is now a lost art in the age of stand-alone songs that are expected to be mixed and matched across any personal playlist. It's not better or worse, just different, and begs for explanation when Zeppelin songs like "Celebration Day" are removed from their original context.

"Since I've Been Loving You" is the slow-blues apex of Zeppelin's entire catalog. They began the climb on "You Shook Me" and "I Can't Quit You Baby." And after *Led Zeppelin III*, they returned from the peak with "Tea for One." In the post-Zeppelin years, Page would continue the journey with "Prison Blues" (from his 1988 solo album *Outrider*) and "Don't Leave Me This Way" from the 1993 *Coverdale-Page*), but he never captured the passion and brilliant musicianship present in "Since I've Been Loving You." This is the kind of achievement only available to a working band of musicians who have lived, traveled, fought, smoked, drank, and performed with each other for years. For a thorough discussion of "Since I've Been Loving You," see "A Closer Look" below.

The last song of side 1 on *Led Zeppelin III* is the hard-rocking "Out on the Tiles" that serves as a formidable bookend to "Immigrant Song" as the album's opener. As Jason Bonham explained on the VH1 television show "Supergroup," the main riff of "Tiles" is based on a limerick his father used to sing about going out to the pubs for a bit of fun. Page took Bonham's melody, Plant added a new lyric, and one of Zeppelin's heaviest rocking songs was created. The band seldom played the song except for the introduction, which was used to launch into "Black Dog" in later years. This lack of recognition from the band has relegated "Tiles" to the status of "deep cut," which is a designation disc jockeys assign to worthy songs buried on an album that only committed fans know about. The main riff is overly complex compared to the older

"Good Times Bad Times" and played too rigidly next to the upcoming "Black Dog," but "Tiles" is still a good romp as Plant sings "a train that's passin' my way helps the rhythm move along."

Led Zeppelin III is an album with two distinct personalities divided by the two sides of the LP. Side 1, with only "Friends" as the exception, is considered the heavy half while side 2, with little reliance on electric guitars, is the soft half. Once you become familiar with the album, you play the side that aligns with your mood. That's how it worked in the 1970s anyway, when the prime choice of music delivery was a vinyl record. And side 2 is all about mellowing out to acoustic sounds and folk-like lyrics drifting from the Welsh countryside. "Gallows Pole" is the lead track and sets a somber tone with minor chords and a lyric that tells the sad tale of a treacherous hangman. Plant rearranged the words from the many other versions of this traditional folk song while Page, Jones, and Bonham laid down a stunning musical backdrop. The rhythm dances through the multiple verses with each adding more instruments and depth as the suspense of the lyric increases. This is about as heavy as a soft song can be.

In April of 1968, the original Yardbirds completed their last recording session while in New York and one of the demos they put down is the unreleased "Knowing That I'm Losing You." Despite Page's attempt to keep the song in the archives, it makes an occasional appearance on the Internet and it is basically a first draft for what would become "Tangerine" on *Led Zeppelin III*. Page takes solo credit as songwriter and there's little doubt the music was his. The recording by the Yardbirds features several guitar overdubs (even the solo) that exactly foreshadow the Zeppelin rendition called "Tangerine." However, the first verse and chorus is completely different and that's a good thing because the Yardbirds' version of the chorus is a shambles. The second verse appears in both versions, leaving speculation as to the songwriting contribution of Keith Relf. But for now, it's all attributed to Page with the help of Plant, who tenderly interprets a lyric about lost love. And thank goodness the citrus-inspired chorus on "Tangerine" has nothing to do with the lemon reference on *Led Zeppelin II*.

If the sweet sentiments of "Tangerine" aren't enough to convince you that Zeppelin has a romantic side, "That's the Way" leaves no doubt. Unlike "Tangerine," which was a Page-only composition, "That's the Way" was a pure Plant-Page collaboration and the difference in the lyric content is striking. Plant beautifully avoids clichés while still conveying a visually and melodically convincing message. With *Led Zeppelin III* in general, and specifically "That's the Way," Plant's prowess as a musical poet is in full bloom. See "A Closer Look" for more discussion of "That's the Way."

In the fall of 1969, Zeppelin visited Olympic studios in London and recorded complete backing tracks to an original song called "Jennings Farm Blues." Lasting over six minutes, this is a substantial composition and Page added multiple electric guitar overdubs complete with solos. The only thing missing was a vocal from Plant. But instead of completing the recording for *Led Zeppelin III*, the track was abandoned and a reworked acoustic version called "Bron-Y-Aur Stomp" was used instead ("Bron-Y-Aur" was a misspelling of the Bron-Yr-Aur cottage visited by Plant and Page). "Jennings Farm Blues" is quite progressive for the timeframe and compared to the softer collection found on *Led Zeppelin III* would have been a high point of the album, assuming Plant would have constructed a nondetrimental melody and lyric. But, inspired by the lack of electricity at the Welsh cottage, they favored the acoustic qualities of "Bron-Y-Aur Stomp" featuring Jones on the fretless bass and Bonham on spoons and castanets. Plant's lyrics "As we walk down a country lane, we'll be singin' a song; hear me call your name" refer not to a girl in hand but to his blue-eyed dog Strider at his side.

On "Hats Off to (Roy) Harper," Zeppelin ends their third album with a downsized tribute to a friend of the band and singer in the style of a multi-song blues jam played at their concerts. The track features only Page on slide guitar while Plant sings through a tremolo effect and has a distinct end-of-the-night improvisational quality as if they worked out a few ideas ahead of time but basically just rolled tape and let it happen. With Jones and Bonham not involved, Page is able to change his chords and rhythmic feel on the fly and he does so repeatedly. Plant stays right with him with snippets of blues lyrics from songs like "Shake 'Em on Down" from Bukka White (also featuring only guitar and vocals with heavy tremolo). Plant delivers tongue-in-cheek lines as good as any of his influences when he caterwauls, "I gave my baby twenty dollar bill; well if that don't get that woman, I'm sure my shotgun will." Adding his own dash of humor, Page plays a "jazzy" major seventh chord just as the track concludes, which is the very antithesis of gut-bucket blues. The boys know how to have a good time.

A CLOSER LOOK

"Immigrant Song"

In 2012, the achievements of Zeppelin were acknowledged by the Kennedy Center Honors and guest speaker Jack Black had this to say: "They sang songs about love; about Vikings; about Vikings *making* love" which brought the house (including the three surviving band members along with President Obama and his wife Michelle) down with laughter. What might seem a strictly comedic reference was actually well grounded in the band's self-created lore and Black did a fine job capitalizing on the myth. With the rhythmic veracity of Thor himself, Zeppelin forever forged a connection between Norse mythology and heavy metal on the opening track to *Led Zeppelin III*, "Immigrant Song."

"Immigrant Song" is exceptionally brief 2:23 (the shortest of all their studio-recorded songs except the acoustic guitar features "Bron-Yr-Aur" and "Black Mountain Side") but the complete ethos of hard rock is packed into its confines. The opening moments feature the atypical combination of only guitar and drums as Page and Bonham establish the pounding riff that anchors the song. At 0:10, Plant enters with an upwardly sweeping wail that further burnished his reputation as the rock singer to beat. Notice the tension created by the third note he sings and how that tension is released when the sustained pitch is finally allowed to move. The pitch interval Plant creates with that note is historically known as the "devil in music" because of its dissonant placement in relation to the musical key set by Page's guitar. Medieval composers took great pains to avoid emphasizing *Diabolus in Musica* and were responsible for the nickname still used today. Plant's use of this interval in such a purposeful manner immediately sets a mood for the recording and brilliantly supports the lyrical subject matter soon to come.

With vivid references to swarthy Nordic life, the first words we hear in "Immigrant Song" are "We come from the land of the ice and snow, from the midnight sun where the hot springs blow." To add more emphasis and fill out the sound, Plant double-tracks the vocals and Jones enters on the bass at the same moment (although, when they performed the song live, Jones did not delay his entrance). As quoted in

Chris Welch's *Led Zeppelin Dazed and Confused,* Plant had this to say about his lyrical inspiration:

> We weren't being pompous. . . .We did come from the land of the ice and snow. We were guests of the Icelandic government on a cultural mission. We were invited to play a concert in Reykjavik and the day before we arrived all the civil servants went on strike and the gig was going to be cancelled. The university prepared a concert hall for us and it was phenomenal. The response from the kids was remarkable and we had a great time. "Immigrant Song" was about that trip and it was the opening track on the album that was intended to be incredibly different.

Even more so than the lemon reference on *Led Zeppelin II,* the very next lyric in "Immigrant Song" would have a lasting impact on the band's legacy: "The hammer of the gods will drive our ships to new lands, to fight the horde, singing and crying, Valhalla I am coming." The entire line is awash in the obvious analogies between long-ship invaders and hedonistic rockers on tour busses, but the expression "hammer of the gods" was singled out and soon became popular with fans and journalists to describe the sound of Zeppelin's thunderous music. Just as "sheets of sound" was used to define John Coltrane, or "slow hand" defined Clapton, so too Zeppelin acquired their convenient (if not overused) catchphrase.

The song moves on to a second section at 0:43 ("On we sweep with threshing oar") where we can hear the aggressive double-time playing of Jones as he propels us toward the jarring halt at 0:50. In a moment that sounds as if Jones and Page could both have fallen forward if they waited any longer to return, the primary riff kicks off again to save the day. By now we start to recognize that more care has been put into the recording production of "Immigrant Song" compared to the simplicity of "You Shook Me" or even "Lemon Song." The multiple layers of Page's guitars are cleanly played; Jones's bass has a particularly burly sound that was not featured at all on their first album and only occasionally on the second ("Heartbreaker," for example); Bonham's drums are prominent and crisp; and Plant's strategic use of double tracking greatly enhances the higher portions of the melody (the live versions of "Immigrant Song" on *How the West Was Won* or the *BBC Sessions* reveal how Plant was pushed to his limits when singing this tune).

At 0:52, the song essentially hits the reset button and we hear a duplicate of the music to that point with only a portion of the lyric changing. The band has already arrived at the charge toward the finish line by 1:39 when the main riff is played mostly unabated to the end. Here Plant provides us a bit of Viking humor by suggesting that despite being sacked and ravaged, it will all be better in the morning: "So now you better stop and rebuild all your ruins 'cause peace and trust can win the day despite all your losing." But as we've heard in Zeppelin songs before, Page is not content to just ramble to the ending without a sonic twist. Listen for the dissonant chord he and Jones play every two measures of music (1:50, 1:55, 1:59 for three examples). Providing unity to the entire recording, this chord is based off the same devil's interval heard in Plant's wailing call to arms during the introduction. Page then employs one more compositional technique to increase the energy of the music without simply turning up the volume. Instead of playing the dissonant chord every two measures, beginning at 2:05 he and Jones switch to playing it at the end of *every* measure and do so until the end of the song. This is a subtle but effective way of putting more wind into the sails of their heavy-metal voyage as the rockers conclude their pillaging.

"Since I've Been Loving You"

Placed as the fourth song on *Led Zeppelin III*, "Since I've Been Loving You" is not only the strongest track on the album, but also one of the band's greatest recorded achievements and even a benchmark in the history of rock music. Based on an extrapolation of a blues progression, "Since" captures a nearly live recording in which all members of the band deliver superb performances that will serve as rock-music templates for as long as music rocks. The song was recorded early in the sessions for the album and includes only minimal overdubbing of a guitar solo added later. Even the bass guitar was omitted in favor of Jones's organ foot pedals so that he could play the keyboard simultaneously with Bonham and Page. Because "Since" was essentially a live recording, the tune became a powerhouse feature for years of concert touring because Zeppelin was able to consistently recreate the authenticity of the studio recording. Audiences responded favorably to the fact that as good as the album version was, the representations on stage matched it step for step. Although we will focus on the original record-ing from *Led Zeppelin III*, several excellent concert renditions of "Since" can be heard on *BBC Sessions, The Song Remains the Same, How the West Was Won,* and *Celebration Day.* Plant and Page also performed the song together in the mid-1990s and a stirring live version with a string orchestra is available on their *No Quarter* album.

It takes Page only five unaccompanied notes to establish the param-eters for what you are about to hear. Hit "stop" just after the opening phrase and ponder what you just heard. The pitches, taken from what guitarists know as the "blues" or "pentatonic" scale, suggest we will be hearing something stripped down and mournful. The slow, deliberate pulse of the notes tells you that Page and company will be in no hurry to convey their story. The middle three notes receive their own rhythmic accent, suggesting the "triplet" feel often used in slow blues. And the cutting timbre of Page's guitar reveals an undercurrent of aggression and excitement. He is reminding us that this is not pop music in which instrumental introductions hastily retreat in sight of a vocalist. Rather, this is rock music in which the guitar is on equal footing to the vocals and no one dares question if Page wants to take thirty seconds or three minutes to enmesh the listener in a new song. Having been duplicated in thousands of bands since, keep in mind that in 1970 this "guitarist and singer as equals" concept was still cutting edge for rock groups and no one at the time was sure where it would all end up. And all of this information is available in just the first five notes of a recording that lasts well over seven minutes.

Push "play" and let us continue. The first twenty-five seconds of "Since I've Been Loving You" could hardly be more minimalistic as far as rock-band instrumentation. No chords are heard. We get only a solo line of notes from Page on guitar while Jones stomps out single bass notes on his foot pedals. This transparent presentation contains such well-chosen notes that even though we are only hearing two single-note lines, complete chords are implied and our ears are satisfied to fill in any missing elements. Yet, if you are listening on earbuds or high-fidelity stereo equipment your ears will also detect an odd sound that doesn't belong. It was hardly audible on the original LP record but with digitally remastered versions available since 1990, the repetitive squeak of John Bonham's bass drum foot pedal is nearly impossible to miss. It is present on several Led Zeppelin recordings but usually easy to ignore because of the density of the arrangements, but here on the opening progression of "Since" the aural artifact stands out against the bare essence of the trio: a guitar solo, a wicked bass line, and the world's greatest rock drummer laying down a brutally simple (and yes, squeaky) beat.

After twenty-five seconds, Jones finally allows for his right hand to make a combination of stabbed and sustained contacts with his keyboard that conjures a brooding quality due to the preponderance of what are called "minor" chords. The trio of Page, Jones, and Bonham has not technically gotten louder, but with the addition of the organ, there is a sensation that the sound is getting heavier. Then, at 0:48 with the flick of a switch on the guitar, Page shifts to an angrier tone that suggests a deadly sharpened saber is now out of the scabbard. Soon after, we hear an enthusiastic "Oh!" as our first hint that Plant is in the room but he's not ready to fully reveal himself just yet. Page is still in control as he charges into a melody rife with statuesque bravado at 0:55.

After pausing briefly, Page returns softly at 1:07 to play a melody that is used throughout the recording to denote the end of each progression and "turnaround" for another pass through the chord cycle. This melody consists of two sets of five notes, and for each set Jones lowers the bass one pitch as he drives toward the "key center" of the entire composition. This descending harmonic cadence is prominent throughout classical music of the eighteenth and nineteenth centuries and a staple of twentieth-century jazz, but far less typical in rock. In isolation, the two chords being used for this figure verge on sounding "pretty" but Page and Jones give it an applicable home in this blues-based rocker. This is only one of several ways the two former recording-session gurus made use of atypical chords in "Since."

Only after a full one minute and fourteen seconds do we hear from Plant in earnest when he treats us to a classic blues-inspired lyric of "Workin' from seven to eleven every night really makes life a drag, and I don't think that's right." But listen to his utter confidence in delivering each sentence fragment. A few words and then a pause. A few more, another pause (during which, the foot pedal continues to squeak). And he gives *drag* a meaningful emphasis by concluding the phrase on a note that creates a subtle tension against the chord of the moment. Although these delivery choices heard in Plant's singing were the result of hundreds of performances where he experimented and learned his craft, we are still swayed by the thought that he is blissfully improvising his melodies in real time rather than studiously pre-composing them. We feel like we are being told a personalized story for the first time, and the storyteller is entirely compelling.

During this opening verse, the band has consciously shifted to act as accompaniment for the vocal. Jones and Plant have removed themselves from the foreground, knowing they will return soon enough. For now, the focus is entirely on Plant as he tells us he's "really been the best of fools." At 2:02 we hear a new chord that begins a crucial point of momentum. For a moment, ignore Plant's voice and listen only to the music. Do you sense how the chords are driving ahead, leading you somewhere? If the song were to end abruptly during this progression we would feel stunted as if we were to find the final pages of a thrilling book to be missing. Now return to Plant's voice and hear his contribution to propel the motion forward. He declares that he will absolutely lose his "worried mind" without his woman's love and we hear the gut-wrenching sincerity in his wailing "ah yeah" at 2:16. This is quickly followed by the band telegraphing via the "turnaround" progression their intention to tell us more.

For the second verse the energy is increased by both Plant and Page. The vocalist kicks off the lyric "Everybody trying to tell me that you didn't mean me no good" at a higher pitch level than used in the opening verse. Like a minister in a Baptist church, Plant is ramping up the message and keeping your attention. Meanwhile, Page begins rolling up and down the notes of each chord in what are called "arpeggios." His volume is still subdued, but the increase in activity has an effect. This elevation continues through 2:50 when Plant tells us with great emotion that he "really did the best" he could, at which time the band does something all too rare in rock music; they get quieter again. Page stops the arpeggios and Plant returns to his lower voice when he revisits his opening line of "I've been working from seven." But the trap has been set. We soon sense the band is only toying with us. Plant uses the final word of "It really makes my life a drag" as a launching pad before exploding into the hook of the song at 3:17 when he wails in his higher register, "Since I've been loving you, yeah." We are here made fully aware of the poignancy of that statement within the story and nod agreeably that the song has been correctly titled.

After this powerful uptick, the trio of Page, Jones, and Bonham once again pull back the throttle slightly as they move through the turn-around progress. But they only drop to about 75 percent of their previous volume so to not lose too much momentum as Page rips open into one of his most riveting solos ever caught on tape. Page features himself throughout an entire verse and the level of musical maturity shown in his improvisation belies his youthful twenty-six years of age. Someone that young simply isn't expected to have this much depth and guts in their playing. For one example, locate the colorful descending riff he plays at 4:04. The world's best rock guitarists could work collectively for days and not come up with a line that interesting and passionate, and Page doesn't stop there. He continues on at 4:10 by showing that brilliance is not about technical speed. Instead, he simply takes a few notes and repeats them several times in a pattern that crosses in and out of the rhythm set by Bonham. It is Page who is now the storyteller and his soul is laid bare to anyone willing to listen. He continues on with some fast picking through the "blues scale" bag of tricks common to many guitarists but he returns once again to a classic Page moment at 4:33. While Jones lays down the "forward momentum" chords on the organ, the guitarist delivers a melody worthy of being developed into a completely separate composition. Then at 4:45, during the descending turn-around chords, Page prepares us for the end of his solo by once again repeating a brief melodic phrase before slamming home the final note at 4:54 where the band comes to a complete halt.

This would be an acceptable moment for Zeppelin to let us catch our breath but it's not going to happen. Instead, Plant charges back to the forefront with a trademark wail that starts high and falls low during the words "Said I been crying, yeah." Only now do our boys in the band take a collective moment to relax while Plant calmly relates how his tears "fell like rain." It is Bonham who first tells us this respite won't last as he brings down a violent three-hit fill on his drums and drags us toward the dramatic final verse.

As Plant cries out that his lover had the nerve to tell him she would be leaving, Page returns to playing the high-energy arpeggios but this time Bonham contributes to the foray by shifting from a steady pattern played on the hi-hat to the fuller sound of his ride cymbal. And in a move typical of Zeppelin, they come up with one more way to highlight the end of a song by deviating from precedents heard earlier in the recording. At 5:45 we hear Plant make a classic blues reference that he opens up his front door only to hear another man slip out the back. This sad state of affairs is supported by Jones and Page, who start off playing the same brooding chord always used at that point of the progression. But listen to the sudden bright shift at 5:52 during the lyric "I must have one of them newfangled back door men." In an unexpected use of a centuries-old compositional device, Page and Jones substitute a major chord for the minor version used in all of the previous verses. Don't the clouds seem to open up at this moment? This victory of "light over dark" while Plant makes what is essentially a punch line delivers a statement heard often in the best of blues themes that even though things are awful at the moment, it's all likely to work out further on down the road.

To provide "Since" a grander sense of journeying forth only to return home somewhat wiser, Plant reminds us one more time at 6:00 that he has been working from seven to eleven and it still makes his life a "drag, drag, drag." But to put the depth of his blues-despair well over the top, the vocalist stretches to one of the highest notes he hits on any recording as he climbs and cascades through the words "Ah, yeah, it makes me drag." Plant then takes a lead from 1960s rhythm and blues singers such as James Brown and Otis Redding, who were known for passionately collapsing on stage only to miraculously reach for the microphone in a valiant attempt to finish a song. As Page, Jones, and Bonham move through the closing sequence of chords, Plant bursts forth at 6:39 with the plea of "just one more, just one more" and the band obliges by backing up for one final approach. This allows Plant to tell us for the last time, "Since I've been loving you, I'm gonna lose my worried mind." Utterly spent, the storyteller steps aside as Bonham guides the musicians home with a series of fills that deliver us to a final rendering of the turnaround figure. The last jazz-inspired chord is struck and staggers back and forth for a moment before dwindling into the faint trickle of organ.

"That's the Way"

Bombastic. Reckless. Trenchant. Relentless. These terms conveniently describe the Zeppelin stereotype but are inadequate to explain the band's more delicate work such as "The Rain Song," "All of My Love," and, from the eclectic *Led Zeppelin III*, "That's the Way." In fact, it is reasonable to label the mood of this recording as downright lovely: a designation not often afforded to pioneers of the heavy metal sound. Other groups from the same period were as important as Zeppelin was to the development of hard-rock idioms, but when considering the early work of Black Sabbath, Blue Cheer, or Deep Purple, the word *lovely* does not apply. Zeppelin did not write ballads in the style that would permeate the albums of 1980s "hair bands" such as Poison and Warrant, but they did write several songs that were slow, nonheavy, and with lyrics that at least suggested (if only cryptically) love both lost and found.

"That's the Way" is dominated by the bright sound of Page's acoustic guitar with the addition of other nonelectric instruments including the pedal steel guitar and dulcimer. This organic sound sprang from its compositional origins in the back hills of Wales while Page and Plant took a break on a walk together. Page had been experimenting with an unusual tuning of his guitar and played an idea for Plant, who quickly came up with a first verse and the two set to work finishing the song.

Picture yourself walking a quiet mile through the Welsh countryside in the summer of 1970 and you detect the echoing sounds of an acoustic guitar and singing wordsmith emanating from a nearby ravine. Moving closer to the sound's source, you hear the opening strains as the guitarist rhythmically strums full, ringing chords. The pace is steady and obvious but deliberately patient. The vocalist then sets an evocative mood with his opening phrase of "I don't know how I'm gonna tell you, I can't play with you no more." Is the reference made between a man and woman? Two children? Or something more literal to musicians such as one bandmate to another? Fortunately, he sings in a relaxed lower register, making sure the enunciation of the lyric is not overshadowed by vocal histrionics. Unfortunately, the subsequent line "I don't know how I'm gonna do what mamma told me, my friend the boy next door" reveals little. About thirty seconds into the music, there is a pause between vocal stanzas and you have a moment to notice the ever-present droning pitch (in this case a G flat) that serves as a harmonic bed while the chords shift languorously just above. Drones have the ability to sedate a listener and Jimmy Page takes full advantage of the effect. As Plant delivers the next lyric, "I can't believe what people saying; you gonna let your hair hang down" you notice a hint of Mick

Jagger–esque street talk in the phrasing that sounds more like "letcha hair hang down." And in further confirmation that the main character within the song is indeed speaking to a woman of personal interest, Plant plaintively asks, "And when I see you out walking, why don't your eyes see me?" You feel the heavy heart as you hear "Could it be you've found another game to play?" Plant's use of such directed language leaves you feeling somewhat voyeuristic to his intimate expressions. After nearly one minute and fifty seconds of being comforted by the ongoing drone, you find the first deviation in the guitar to be alarming but the shift allows the singer to introduce you to the "hook" of the lyric while he knows your attention is rapt. You learn that whatever changes and loss our protagonist faces, he might find solace in knowing "that's the way" things were meant to be. Not great poetry perhaps, but when delivered in the context of the singer's melody and guitarist's harmony, the message conveys sincere warmth. Driving home the main point that mother knows best, the vocalist finally slips up to a high note (for most male rock singers) at 2:00 to emphasize the statement, "Mama said that's the way it oughta stay." At 2:10 you hear the guitarist working his way back to the opening progression and it is only now that you notice how the energy and tension have been gradually increasing for the full two minutes. Plant and Page have successfully melded the lyrical topic with the musical texture to this point in a manner equal to any text-painting composer of the Renaissance. The music and words seem so well matched that it becomes impossible to imagine them unmarried.

The next verse presents the pastoral imagery of rivers, fish, flowers, and tearful maidens but at 2:50 you begin to sense a growing agitation even though the words are peaceful and the chords have not changed. Oddly, the guitarist has increased the pulse just enough that it would be obvious when compared side by side to the tempo of the opening minutes. Page would increase the tempo within a famous yet-to-be-written ballad rocker ("Stairway to Heaven") as a purposeful effect but there is nothing in the words or structural arch of "That's the Way" to support the increased pace so it must be assumed that it is simply an inadvertent performance error a musician might make when playing without a drummer such as Bonham to lock in a beat. Returning to the music, you choose to overlook the faux pas and are drawn to the singer's wordless vocalizations and folksy tambourine while the guitarist improvises twisting and sliding melodies over the now-familiar drone. After nearly five and a half minutes, the pleasing blend of voice and guitar begins to fade as if the duo has begun to saunter further up the valley and out of earshot. But while you were there in that suspended moment of artistic creation, the music performed by two mates known more for volume and bombast was nothing if not lovely.

4

ONE SONG TO BIND THEM ALL

As a response to journalists who were hell bent on attacking anything with the band's name on it, Led Zeppelin released their fourth album in November 1971 with no title at all. The only distinctive markings on the album cover were four symbols, each representing a member of the band. The ambiguity has generated many adopted names over the years, including "The Stairway Album," *Zoso* (an approximation of Page's symbol), *Untitled*, the "Four Symbols" album, or the safely precedented *Led Zeppelin IV*. Definitive title aside, the album stormed the charts, forever changing the band's future and legacy. As it stands, the album contains a collection of notable songs such as "Black Dog," "When the Levee Breaks," and "Going to California," but it is the slow burn to heavy scorch found in "Stairway to Heaven" that fans have consistently embraced with cultic fervor. The adventurous FM-radio disc jockeys of the day played the lengthy song more than any other Zeppelin track and it soon became the staple for the last dance at every middle and high school dance in America for the next decade and beyond. In the years following *Led Zeppelin IV*, nothing would ever be the same for the band or any of its members.

After the preponderance of acoustic songs on *Led Zeppelin III*, fans of the band's heavier side were hoping the next album would cater more to their tastes. You only have to hear the first song to know such concerns were allayed. "Black Dog" embraces the very essence of hard rock, or at least what we think the essence should be. Ideally there should be wailing vocals: check. A killer riff: check. A searing guitar solo: check. And lyrics about girls but nothing too romantic: check and check. For a closer look into "Black Dog," see below.

"Rock and Roll" is the second song on *Led Zeppelin IV* and further confirms that the band has their blood up. Bonham counts off the song with a freight-train introduction that sounds ready to come off the rails at any moment. Jones and Page just barely manage to catch the rhythm and lay down a classic rock and roll groove for Plant to kick out one of his impossibly high melodies; so high that he often changed it in concert to something more manageable. There's nothing overtly original about "Rock and Roll" as a song. It's really just homage to the roots of a genre and Zeppelin is taking a moment to blow off some steam while offering a tip of the hat to those who came before them. For a closer look into a live rendition of "Rock and Roll" from 2007, see chapter 10.

"The Battle of Evermore" is one of the very few Zeppelin tracks to engage an outside musician and the only time for a vocalist. Although Page plays an active mandolin throughout the track (his first time using the instrument), "Battle" is primarily a vocal feature for Plant with assistance from Sandy Denny, who at times melds her voice so seamlessly into Plant's that it's hard to distinguish the two. In general, Denny serves as an eye witness to immediate danger when she sings warnings like "throw down your plow and hoe; rest not to lock your homes" while Plant is the omnipotent narrator telling a story such as "I hear the horses thunder down in the valley below; I'm waiting for the angels of Avalon, waiting for the eastern glow." There were times male vocalists like David Coverdale or Paul Rogers could match the dynamic power of Plant, but the Zeppelin singer had all his contemporaries beat when it comes to writing poetic imagery free of cliché or obvious symbolism and lazy rhymes. The man can write.

Zeppelin had been performing "Stairway to Heaven" in the months leading up to the release of the record so they already had a good feeling about how the song would be received. Audiences enthusiastically responded to hearing the new song and Zeppelin hoped that reaction would transfer to their record-buying fans and that's exactly what happened. There was so much interest in the song that Atlantic Records pleaded with Zeppelin to release an edited version as a single. The band declined. If you wanted to own a copy, you had to buy the complete album. And to this day, *Led Zeppelin IV* is still one of the best-selling albums in the world with an estimated 37 million sales. For a closer look at "Stairway to Heaven," see below.

"Misty Mountain Hop" starts off side 2 of *Led Zeppelin IV* with a jaunty electric piano progression that cozies up to music for the merry-go-round, but Bonzo and Page enter soon enough with a tough edge and heavy hand. There's a rare mistake from Jones on the keyboards around 2:10 but the ensemble (especially Bonham) sounds so good throughout the track that they didn't bother trying to fix it. The song title is the second Tolkien reference on the album (the other being a "ring wraith" in "The Battle of Evermore") although the lyrics don't linger in Middle Earth. Rather, they hang out with a groovy congregation at the park, when Plant sings, "Crowds of people sittin' on the grass with flowers in their hair said, 'Hey boy, do you wanna score?'" Plant, being one with people, responds with a wink, "And you know how it is."

"Four Sticks" is one of the most adventurous songs Zeppelin ever recorded. The main riff is comprised of notes that don't normally get played together by a hard-rock band and their use gives the music an exotic quality. The exoticism is further enhanced by the mixed time signatures that often include only five beats in a measure. These peculiarities caused considerable challenges for Bonham in the studio and out of frustration he grabbed a second pair of drum sticks and that was how he got through the successful take. It is only fitting that the song title acknowledges his zealous solution. Of note is the appearance at 3:00 of Jones playing a rare VCS3 synthesizer that is known for having incredibly unreliable pitch. True to its reputation, the instrument wavers and fades away after thirty seconds.

Listen carefully to the beginning of "Going to California" and enjoy the sound of Plant inhaling a quick hit of air. Being that the opening lyric is "Spent my days with a woman unkind; smoked my stuff and drank all my wine," we can make a fair assumption for what he was inhaling. Had this song been on *Led Zeppelin III* it would have been a nice addition. But among the harder-edged collection on *Led Zeppelin IV* it is a golden revelation. Anyone that's ever journeyed west into a sunset can relate to "Made up my mind to make a new start; going to California with an aching in my heart." And in a tone of sweet optimism, Plant sings, "Standing on a hill in my mountain of dreams; telling myself it's not as hard, hard, hard as it seems." California serves as his metaphor for resolving any crisis when someone moves your cheese.

Look to west, inhale, and he'll "meet you up there where the path runs straight and high."

The sound of power emanating from Bonham's drumming on "When the Levee Breaks" is the stuff of legend. But that achievement shouldn't overshadow the killer groove laid down by Page and Jones. And Plant sings like a bluesman possessed by his deepest anguish after a long night of whiskey, women, and bad decisions. The track lasts a long seven minutes but leaves us wanting more. The drone-like quality of the relentless riff reaches into your gut and demands attention. You might refuse, but saying "yes" just feels better. For a closer look at "Levee," see below.

A CLOSER LOOK

"Black Dog"

The most impressive aspect of one of Zeppelin's most impressive tunes is the drum playing of John Bonham. "Black Dog" is immediately recognized for its call-and-response structure, high and bluesy vocals, and intricate riffs that form the song's backbone, but the drumming should not be overlooked. Jones was the primary songwriter for the piece and sought to create a riff that would be difficult for other bands to cover. To accomplish this, he used mixed time signatures that intimidate less advanced musicians. It sounds like they drop a beat somewhere, so to play along, you are forced to "mess up" in order to get it right. The problem was to present this configuration in a manner that still flowed naturally and sounded like Zeppelin rather than their progressive-rock contemporaries Yes or Emerson, Lake, and Palmer. While other drummers of the period would likely have not withstood the seduction of Jones's complex riffs, Bonham concluded that the most elegant solution was to simply play a solid, steady rock beat, knowing that eventually the mixed meter would come back around to him. This is analogous to the old joke that even the hands on a busted clock are correct twice a day. There is a moment or two where Bonham appears out of sync with Page and Jones, but with a little patience, they soon intersect on the same beat.

In 1969, Fleetwood Mac had success with "Oh Well" in which they alternate between a vocal line and a rhythmically interesting riff. But Fleetwood Mac fell prey to a common problem with bands that didn't have a Robert Plant of their own: the vocals of Peter Green appear inconsequential next to instrumental portions of the song. It sounds as if they only tolerated just enough vocals to provide the tune a lyrical hook and get it on the radio.

Zeppelin, however, had no reason to downplay their vocalist or the lyrics he contributed to "Black Dog." While Green got around to singing the self-deprecating "I can't help about the shape I'm in; I can't sing, I ain't pretty and my legs are thin" after forty-five seconds, Plant attacked from the very opening as an alpha dog with the sexually charged "Hey, hey mama say the way you move, gonna make you sweat, gonna make you groove." Plant's melody notes are all taken from the blues scale and he sings in a register high enough to ward off pale imitators (even Plant had to lower the key when performing this song in later decades). The band then hammers away at the first appearance of the main riff in all its glory. Both Page and Jones play the same line of single notes together and Page went even further to maximize the sound by recording three different guitar parts all playing the same riff (called "triple tracking"). And laying down an unwaveringly solid groove is Bonham, who chooses a rhythm that is half the pace of the guitars. This contrast is classic Bonham who was one of the few rock drummers capable of generating more intensity by playing less. While Page and Jones seem to pick away furiously, Bonham just grooves along right in the rhythmic pocket.

The call of Plant and the response of the three-piece rhythm section continues and if you listen very hard during the vocal portions you will hear the occasional click of drum sticks. Bonham was keeping time for the band during their pauses and the noise was not entirely muted from the track later on. After forty seconds, the band continues beyond the length of the main riff by transposing it to another pitch and this is where things get interesting. Listen how the rhythm of the notes falls back on itself in a slightly awkward way. And yet, with Bonham's insistent groove, the players of "Black Dog" all remain firmly grounded. Moving on at 0:53, we hear a new idea that would function as a vocal chorus in the midst of many other rock songs, but Zeppelin (especially Page) avoided the verse-chorus structure as often as possible. Instead,

Page leads the charge with a spirited guitar figure while Plant simply sings "oh yeah" several times. Not a very inspired lyric to be sure, but this designates even more weight to the words in the call and response sections.

Arriving at 1:05, we get another dose of Plant doing all he can to perpetuate his stature as the insatiable rocker on the road when he sings, "I gotta roll, can't stand still, got a flaming heart, can't get my fill." This was an image Plant played out nightly on stage with his open shirt, tight jeans, and flowing golden tresses (the photo on the cover of this book is a prime example). The next lyric contains the only correlation to the song title. "Eyes that shine burning red" can be visually associated with a dog although in reality the name "Black Dog" was little more than a reference to an animal seen hanging around the studio during the recording sessions.

At 1:26, Plant sings, "ah, ha," in two pitches that move downward followed by the same two words but with the pitches moving up. This is the audience participation portion of "Black Dog" and if you were one of the exuberant fans at a 1970-something concert you and tens of thousands of your rocking brethren would have sung the second group of notes at the direction of Plant. But in the recording studio he is left to do the work without you. Then, with an upward sweep of his vocals, Plant delivers us to yet another new section of the song.

The fresh material at 1:40 is strong enough that it could be the chorus of its own song but it is used here as a bridge or transition. Plant sings a handful of variations on the word *baby* but is content to let much of the music go by with no vocals at all. Other rock bands could write songs for years not stumbling across such a strong musical phrase while Zeppelin, in their youthful confidence, are willing to toss it off as an extra riff in a song already shimmering with riches.

At this point, the band basically resets itself to play a duplicate of everything we've heard to this point but with new lyrics and a few textural additions. Another call-and-response sequence begins at 2:04 with a further smattering of drum-stick clicks while Plant intones blues references to evil, swarthy women with lyrics like "I don't know but I been told, a big-legged woman ain't got no soul." Zeppelin works their way through another playing of the beat-dropping riff and first pseudo-chorus but Page surprises us with a new addition after Plant returns for another volley of call and response. After the line "All I ask for when I pray, steady rollin' woman gonna come my way," listen at 3:07 to hear a new guitar part playing the main riff but in a harmony that is higher. Page loves to add little touches of orchestration like this and it's easy to picture him spending considerable time hearing these notes in his head and figuring them out on the fret board of his instrument. He liked this harmony part so much that when Zeppelin performed "Black Dog" in concert he would always choose the alternate line over the main riff at this section of the song knowing Jones would still supply the latter.

Plant takes us through one more audience-participation section before stepping aside to the let the band thunder away using the pseudo-chorus #2 material but this time Page unleashes a fiery solo. A notable component of several Page solos is his willingness to echo his own ideas. Less developed improvisers often feel pressured to keep churning out fresh sequences of notes, but Page's work as a session player taught him the value of repetition. Simply put, if it sounds good once, playing it a couple more times won't hurt. There are several examples of this concept throughout Page's "Black Dog" solo but one worth noting is the opening phrase at 3:38. He begins with an upward flurry of notes only to repeat them two more times. He then releases the repetitive tension with a new line of notes that moves generally downward. Liking what he hears, Page then repeats the entire sequence again at 3:43. The remainder of his solo is not as structured, but after listening a few times you will begin to appreciate how Page's mind was constantly working through multiple ideas and employing a musical version of economy in motion.

"Stairway to Heaven"

In the farcical romp that is the *Wayne's World* movie, Mike Myers portrays the rock-worshiping man on the street and in a brilliant scene at a music store he begins to play a few rolling notes on a guitar only to be quickly admonished by a salesman, who points to a sign reading, "No Stairway to Heaven." Any guitar store employee since the early 1970s can appreciate the humor as Myers says, "No Stairway? Denied." In another pop-culture reference, on an episode of the late-1980s television show *Moonlighting*, lead actor Bruce Willis is asked if he has any requests before the bad guys are going to rub him out. With his trademark grin he responds, "The long version of 'Stairway to Heaven.'"

Sometimes a song transcends all original intentions until it becomes de facto property of the masses. Zeppelin gave birth to a few nice chords, some thoughtful arranging, an epic solo, and esoterically attractive lyrics, but they long ago lost control of the beast the sum of the parts became. The song may have been conceived in the quiet of a fireside hearth, but it now belongs to the world, even if that includes the tongue-in-cheek humor of Hollywood actors.

Page had been formulating ideas for a lengthy composition for some time. He was fascinated by the idea of a song that would propel itself forward with very little repetition (classical composers call this technique "through composed"). Portions of what would eventually be called "Stairway to Heaven" were created at the Bron-Yr-Aur cottage in Wales but the disparate pieces were joined together while the band rehearsed at Headley Grange outside of London. While Page, Jones, and Bonham chopped away at the process of pulling the several sections of the song into a cohesive whole, Plant sequestered himself in a corner jotting down lyrics inspired by what he was hearing. When he joined the others they were quite surprised to find he had completed nearly enough lyrics for the entire song, especially the shimmering opening line, "There's a lady who's sure all that glitters is gold and she's buying a stairway to heaven." Later in the evening when Jones and Bonham left for a London pub, Page and Plant stayed behind to thread together some lingering ideas and the song was essentially ready to be recorded.

The first foundational tracks were captured at Island Studios in London with Page on an acoustic guitar, Jones on electric piano, and Bonham on drums. Afterward, the bass was added and then Page began orchestrating his various electric guitars. To add a pastoral quality in support of the lyrical imagery, Jones suggested playing the recorder flute during the introduction, although those parts would eventually be played on keyboards at concerts. And finally, the guitar solo and vocals were added and the song that is often cited as the finest rock ballad of all time was completed. The complete run time was eight minutes: an unheard of length for a studio track that wasn't just based on jamming, and yet far shorter than the fifteen-minute composition Page had been hinting at in interviews. There was really no precedent for a song of this length to become a radio-played hit worldwide, but Zeppelin had a sense that the song was special and began to perform it live even before the release of *Led Zeppelin IV*. Zeppelin was rather bold to ask audiences to accept and rate an unfamiliar song that would stretch out to ten or eleven minutes, but the response was prophetically enthusiastic.

One such pre-release performance was March 5, 1971, at Ulster Hall in Belfast. Had you been there, you would have first been impressed by the classic design of the hall that originally opened in 1862. With seating for a thousand, this is a large venue for the time, and yet can you imagine now the thought of seeing a group with the stature of Led Zeppelin in such an "intimate" setting? Flanked by the pipes of the historically important Mulholland Grand Organ, the band took the stage once used by Charles Dickens. In the 1940s, the venue functioned as a dance hall to entertain the billeted American soldiers ("overpaid, oversexed, and over here" as the locals would say), but on this night it was all about having some escapist fun amid the troubling and sometimes riotous protests gripping Belfast at the time. You would have cheered mightily when the band opened up with the familiar "Immigrant Song" and felt equally as impressed with the riff-based "Black Dog" even though this is the first time you were hearing it. Soon, Zeppelin takes you on a moody improvisational journey through "Dazed and Confused" during which you are treated to Page playing his guitar with a violin bow. Things couldn't be more entertaining and you excitedly await the next classic song that you have heard many times on your turntable. But instead, a voice rises clear above the din as the enigmatic Plant asks for your indulgence while they try out another new piece that would be released on their upcoming album. There is polite but conditional encouragement from those in the hall who privately hope the excursion is kept brief or that the song is immediately accessible like "Black Dog." You find yourself intrigued by Page strapping on a custom-made, double-neck guitar with twelve strings on one neck and six on the other. If Page is admitting that even a guitar wizard like himself needs special equipment to play the next song, there must be something quite unique afoot.

Then it begins. Page sweeps his hand across the twelve-stringed guitar steadily plucking the notes of an A-minor chord. This harmonic "key center" is important in that when the open strings ring empathetically (intentionally or otherwise), they still sound pleasing. Other keys do not always accommodate this phenomenon and the result of choosing A-minor is a fuller, robust sound. Minor keys also create a melancholy timbre and the crowd quiets down in response. After the opening guitar passage, Jones joins on the organ using a fluty sound to approximate the wood recorder used on the album. The simple organ melody and rolling guitar combine to suggest a Renaissance-era quality. You could close your eyes and be transported centuries back in time to a fireside gathering of traveling minstrels who woo the local villagers with wondrous tales from over the hills and far away. The music patiently continues instrumentally while the vocalist waits in the wings. Zeppelin were fully capable of bashing an audience into submission with their unapologetic rockers, but this was an attempt to achieve the same goal through much more difficult means—subtlety.

After nearly a minute, Plant emerges with the opening line that immediately conveys a sense of feminine mysticism and hope: "There's a lady who's sure all that glitters is gold." Within the first stanza Plant mentions the "stairway to heaven" twice so there is no mistaking the likely title of the song. It doesn't take long for you to realize that Plant is not going to hand over an obvious story. That would be too easy. Instead, you hear snippets of post-hippie poetry that invite you to assign meaning from your own life experiences. We are then gifted portents requiring our vigilance. First, we must look closer at signs on the wall because "sometimes words have two meanings." Second, take heed of songbirds that sing "all of our thoughts are misgiven."

You have now been listening to this new Zeppelin composition for over two minutes and you notice Jones shifting from his organ to the electric piano before hearing the music move from the "A" to the "B" section. It would be tempting to equate this to a verse-chorus format, but frankly, the lyrics of B aren't strong enough to warrant the designation of "chorus." Plant just sings in his mellow manner that "it makes me wonder." Maybe it's the effect of pot wafting in the air, but you find yourself nodding in agreement with his simple admission.

Zeppelin then leads you through two more repetitions of A and B as Plant unveils more details by moving into first person with "there's a feeling I get when I look to the west and my spirit is crying for leaving." Then, opening up the lyric to all of you in the theater, he adds, "It's whispered that soon if we all call the tune, then the piper will lead us to reason." Plant has slowly transitioned from the abstract of an unknown woman to the more accessible first person, and then finally delivered the lyrics in your hands with the word *we*. To fully involve you in the developing experience, Plant sings, "and the forests will echo with laughter," but adds an improvised tag by asking with a smile, "Does anyone remember laughter?" You and a thousand of your concert-going friends burst forth in jubilant response.

The song moves on and as Plant sings that you needn't be alarmed by any "bustle in your hedgerow," you are reminded that something has been absent for the first four minutes of music—the drums. Bonham remedies the situation by entering with a slow-paced rock beat for the forthcoming A and B sections. Moving into the fifth minute of music you are beginning to wonder what's coming next and the answer comes with what can accurately be described as fanfare music. The band actually trumpets their own arrival at a portal of transition where they cast off the garb of countryside travelers and reveal themselves as sentinels of rock who wield electrified instruments of imposing power.

You find yourself clapping along to the energy of the tempo during the fanfare but you notice you get thrown off the beat somewhere along the way. This is not surprising because Page created a rhythmically complex figure that sounds deceptively simple. Keeping your eyes on Bonham you notice him struggling to hold the beat with his foot on the hi-hat while he bangs out the syncopations with his hands. He navigates his way through the passage to join the band on the downbeat of the next section but years later when you hear the recording of "Stairway" from *The Song Remains the Same* you'll notice he fumbles enough that Page and Jones have to adjust. But on this night things go exactly as planned even when Zeppelin does something unheard of in rock music: they speed up the tempo on purpose.

Nearly six minutes have passed and the band begins laying down the chord progression for an extended Jimmy Page solo. It was Page who willfully designed the tempo change into his composition. He was convinced that the increase in energy would be exciting enough to override any opinion that they "broke the rules" and he was supported by the mesmerized audience. The slightly faster tempo and the new chord progression provided Page an excellent foundation over which to weave his masterful playing. The three chords used (A minor to G major to F major) are a vehicle used in many rock songs as a jamming section ("All Along the Watchtower," for example) and Page was very familiar with them long before "Stairway" came to be. On the studio recording he limited himself to ten sequences of the chord progression but at concerts he could stretch it for as long as desired based on his mood and the audience reaction. On *The BBC Sessions* he played thirteen. On *How the West Was One* there were an impressive twenty-eight progressions. On *The Song Remains the Same* Page had enough on his musical mind to solo through thirty-six progressions. But on this night in Belfast you aren't bothering to count and just let the improvisation sweep over you as Bonham and Jones adjust and react to the various signals transmitted by their guitarist. To communicate to the band when his solo was finally ending, Page always plays the same, fast and repetitive lick (on *Led Zeppelin IV* you can hear it at 6:43).

Using the same three chords as during the guitar solo, Plant re-emerges to grip the audience with his full rock voice in the upper portions of his range. Embracing the *we* as he had before, he belts out a new melody with the words "As we wind on down the road, our shadows taller than our soul, there walks a lady we all know, who shines white light and wants to show, how everything still turns to gold." Using a mirror writing technique, Plant has now brought us back to the lady we first learned of some seven minutes earlier. Then, in a final burst of hard-rock wisdom, you hear Plant sing, "If you listen very hard, the tune will come to you at last, when all are one and one is all, to be a rock and not to roll." He lets the last word linger and fall away in a mournful call, distracting you from the fact that the last line is pretty corny and not nearly on par with the poetic quality of all that came before.

As Plant's voice trails off, the band plays through the same chord progression a final four times before you hear Bonham pulling hard on the brakes and slowing the heavy-metal train down to a complete stop. All eyes are on Plant as he lifts the microphone and gently sings, "And she's buying a stairway" (pause) "to heaven." The band rumbles lightly on a final A-minor chord while you and the rest of your compatriots unleash a torrent of applause and cheers of approval. You have witnessed rock history in the making. On this night, and for the next few years, when Zeppelin played "Stairway" it was a singular moment shared between the band and the people at the venue. But soon the song would become the most requested on rock stations for the rest of the decade. Soon it would be the theme for proms and birthday parties. Soon it would become the musical albatross around Plant's neck that he would be expected to sing the rest of his life. Soon it would belong to the world. But on the night of March 5, 1971, it felt like Zeppelin was playing just for you and the world would have to wait its turn.

"When the Levee Breaks"

As if the drums on "Black Dog" weren't impressive enough, along comes "When the Levee Breaks" and sets an industry-wide expectation from that moment on as to what rock drums can and should sound like. Whenever a drummer or producer tells a sound engineer she or he wants the "Bonham" sound, it's "Levee" they are talking about. The lads had already attempted to record the song at another location with no usable results but when Bonham was inspired by a just-arrived new drum kit at the Headley Grange recording session, they decided to give it one more try. Rather than record the drums in an enclosed booth with microphones nearby, Page and the audio engineer, Andy Johns, decided to take advantage of a three-story hallway with one of the microphones on the second floor. With the drums placed at the bottom of a staircase, they ran the signal through a guitar echo effect and added a considerable amount of compression to elevate the perceived volume. With this combination of ideas they hit the aural jackpot. This immense audio sound may have come from Johns and Page, but it was Bonham who knew what to do with what he was given. The grinding beat he delivered not only became an iconic Zeppelin moment but also provided fodder to be digitally sampled (not always legally) and emulated by others for decades to come. Without "Levee," grunge musicians of the early 1990s would have needed to dig much deeper for inspiration.

"Levee" opens up with two measures of the best slow-rock drumming you can hope to hear. There is a solid snare-drum back beat (hits on the second and fourth beats) while the kick drum thunders away in between and subdivision on the high hat strings it all together. With each hit of the kick or snare drum, you will notice the immediate slap-back echo that makes Bonham sound like he is playing in a massive auditorium while you are listening in the distant cheap seats. Bonham was known to be dissatisfied with the aural mix of his drums on earlier Zeppelin albums so it's no wonder the band decided to feature him unaccompanied on the introduction to "Levee" once he was pleased with the sound being recorded. Eight seconds later the rest of Zeppelin joins in the groove. While Page and Jones establish a bluesy (and compared to "Black Dog," decidedly not complex) riff, Plant treats us to a rare appearance of his harmonica playing. The note he initially digs into is called a "minor seventh" and the harmonic tension it creates against the key of the music sets an ominous tone that foreshadows the impending subject matter of the lyrics.

Similar to several lyrics on earlier Zeppelin albums, Plant used another artist's work for inspiration, although this time proper credit was given to Memphis Minnie, who recorded a song called "When the Levee Breaks" with her husband, Kansas Joe McCoy, in 1929. Plant's melody and inflections differ from Minnie's but they both open up with the same foreboding prediction, "If it keeps on raining, levee's going to break; and if the levee breaks, I'll have no place to stay." The original "Levee" is based on the chord progression normally found in a twelve-measure blues pattern but Zeppelin deviated from the norm in their version. They simplified the music down to a repetitive riff that never changes underneath Plant's opening verses. In a typical blues progression, the chords move during the restatement of the opening lyric. But in "Levee," Zeppelin doesn't budge from their grinding riff. This creates a drone effect that lulls us into a creeping malaise only to find ourselves jolted when the harmony finally moves at 2:13.

At this point, Page asserts himself with an unaccompanied transitional figure employing several layers of guitar. Unfortunately, he didn't take the time to correct a tuning problem that can be heard around 2:30. Page was also guilty of this offense on the ending of "Babe I'm Gonna Leave You" from *Led Zeppelin* and such obvious missteps are incongruous when considering how meticulous he usually was while producing these albums. But the melodic slip-sliding Page plays on this section is interesting enough for his brief sin to be forgiven and Plant soon returns with a strong chorus-like statement that erases the memory of any recent mistakes.

In the early twentieth century, there was a major migration of blacks in America as they departed the South to find work and a better life in the North, especially Chicago. This diaspora is often reflected in blues lyrics, and in "Levee" Plant embraces the topic when he sings, "If you're goin' down South they got no work to do if you don't know about Chicago." This is a particularly strong lyric combined with an equally potent melody so it would make perfect sense if we were to hear it reappear later in the song but, once again, Zeppelin resists conventional pop songwriting so this potentially memorable chorus is not heard sung again. Instead, Plant picks up the harmonica for another solo passage similar to the lengthy introduction material.

At 4:09, the words "Crying won't help you and praying won't do you no good" are delivered with convincing pithiness as Plant reminds us that weather is the great equalizer answering to no one. But do you notice something different about his voice? In order to create variety from the earlier verse, Page has added a chorus effect to the vocals. When Plant continues at 4:37 with "All last night, sat on the levee and moaned" the effect becomes even deeper. If you jump quickly between this verse and the first, the difference is startling, but because the changes were added gradually through the recording, we hardly notice Page's studio tinkering.

The band leads us back to the chorus-like variation at 5:09 but, as previously divulged, just when we expect to hear vocals similar to the first go-around, Plant treats us to less interesting material simply using the words *ah* and *oh*. While Bonham relentlessly thunders on, Page plays some prominent slide-guitar figures at 5:35 before returning the band to a final droning march through the closing minute of the recording. And not satisfied to borrow from just one source, Plant doubles down on his earlier Northern reference by singing a line from "Going to Chicago" (a blues recorded by artists such as Jimmy Witherspoon, Joe Williams with Count Basie, and T-Bone Walker). Plant mournfully tells his listener, "I'm sorry I can't take you" on his Chicago-bound sojourn. The correlation between the character in his song and the life of a road-warrior rock star is no coincidence. He will give you everything he's got, but sooner or later, he's moving on to give it all to someone else. Listen to the defiant and convincing tone as he digs into the words "I'm going down." This is a man not to be swayed by a mere catastrophic flood. Along with "Since I've Been Loving You," "When the Levee Breaks" was Led Zeppelin at their best reinterpreting American blues into something distinctly their own.

5

THE CONFOUNDED BRIDGE

Throughout *Houses of the Holy* (released in March 1973 and some-times referred to as *Led Zeppelin V*), Led Zeppelin exhibits their more progressive side with songs like "No Quarter" and "The Rain Song." Intricate songwriting far removed from simplistic blues riffs come into full bloom on "The Song Remains the Same" and "Over the Hills and Far Away." In fact, this is the first Zeppelin album to not include at least one song centered on the blues tradition. They were looking to push themselves as songwriters and the blues was too comfortable. By deny-ing themselves a safety net, they wrote an album's worth of songs with intricate harmonies and rhythms (overlooking the simple sock-hop chords in "D'Yer Mak'er"), several of which became perennial entries on concert set lists. *Houses of the Holy* also announces the increased contribution of John Paul Jones as a keyboardist. Armed with new tech-nology (synthesizers and foot pedals), the band had more choices when it came to instrumentation or solos. Jones will always be remembered as the bassist in Led Zeppelin, but when given the opportunity to sit more often at the keyboard, he proves himself to be a dual threat. And casting aside more than ever the trappings of what a "heavy" rock band is expected to play, Zeppelin gives a tip of the hat to the funk of James Brown ("The Crunge") and reggae ("D'yer Mak'er"). *Houses of the Holy* serves as an unmistakable bridge to a new period for the band during which they refused to sink into cliché and derivative self-parody. After four years and five albums, the band is not content to simply produce music echoing their success. The question was, where would this momentum take them?

With "The Song Remains the Same," Zeppelin offers you an overture to a grand instrumental composition that never materialized. For years, Page had been carving away at ideas for a large-scale work, but some of the components were so strong that Plant couldn't resist adding lyrics. Play the opening 1:30 of "The Song Remains the Same" and enjoy some of Page's best guitar orchestration on record. It's hard to imagine how a band that made its bones on riffs as simple as "Whole Lotta Love" could write music as intricate and alluring as the first track on *Houses of the Holy*. And when the tempo finally cuts in half at Plant's entrance, it's like the palace doors are cast open to announce the arrival of an epic hero preparing to address his legions. When Plant sings "I had a dream" in a weary but knowing voice, we believe him and want to know more. After a superior guitar solo, Plant jumps to a new octave with "California starlight, sweet Calcutta rain" as if he just took a hit of helium, but it is the result of the tape being sped up. This proved a difficult melody for Plant to reproduce in later concerts but he often came close. By 2007, Plant lowered the key and considerably rewrote the melody. That's what he gets for insisting on his presence in what was originally intended to be a glorious guitar feature for Page. If you are ever underwhelmed by the slop and chop Page sometimes plays when live in concert, call up a copy of the original "Song Remains the Same" from *Houses of the Holy* and be reminded what a brilliant craftsman he is when able to layer his thoughts together.

"Rain Song" is undoubtedly the most beautiful song Zeppelin ever recorded. The hauntingly earnest guitar, sweeping string parts, and poetically fresh lyrics coalesce to create a revelation in the Zeppelin catalog. Completely abandoning his bread-and-butter riffs for layered chords and melodic contours, Page elevates his songwriting to a new level and the band is both willing and capable of walking at his side. The first two chords, borrowed from George Harrison's "Something," are all you need to hear to know a ballad is coming your way. But instead of moving the song toward a power-chord climax as heard in "Stairway to Heaven," this time Zeppelin uses Plant's vocals and the keyboard-strings of Jones to bring us to fruition. At 7:40, "The Rain Song" is a powerful testament of Zeppelin's ability to maintain our attention in a "rock ballad" when such songs don't typically pass five minutes. Plant closes with a line that might have just as well come from a greeting card, but that doesn't make it less true: "Upon us all a little rain must fall."

By the beginning of the album's third track, "Over the Hills and Far Away," you wonder if Zeppelin isn't delivering another version of *Led Zeppelin III* in which the rocking "Immigrant Song" (the bait) is followed by a majority of acoustic songs (the switch). And while it does take until 1:30 for "Over the Hills" to pick up speed, there's something different about the soul of this song and "The Rain Song" it follows. This is not a folk-inspired walk down a country lane. This is a pensive and elaborate musical journey supported by literary expressions of inner strife. "Many times I've been bitten; many times I've gazed along the open road" Plant sings and we nod our heads in comforting agreement that we've all been there. The funky groove and guitar solo at 2:30 followed by the stair-step transition back to the verse is not to be missed.

For pure rhythmic complexity, Zeppelin is off the charts with "The Crunge." Composed in the studio by all four members, who started jamming over a Bonham groove, there is an obvious connection to the funk of James Brown. Jones has often played active bass lines ("Ramble On" and "What Is and What Should Never Be," for example), but here he delivers his best James Jamerson (a famous soul and funk bassist) impression. Page strums his strings in tight, syncopated rhythms while Plant tells his friends down at the pub about the girl that makes him whirl and twirl. And with that pervasive Plant charm, he claims, "I ain't gonna tell you nothing; I ain't gonna no more, no!" But of course this is promptly followed by a full account of her seductive qualities. And dig, if you will, the pseudo-brass-section figures Jones drops in on the synthesizer. Real brass would have given this track more credibility (something left wanting by the unavoidable heaviness of Zeppelin's playing), but the band kept it simple by staying in the family. If Plant's question, "Where's that confounded bridge?" strikes you as random, it is a reference to James Brown, who often gave on-microphone directions to his band, including moving on to a middle section or "bridge" of a song. In the case of Zeppelin, the punchline is that "The Crunge" has no bridge, confounded or otherwise.

"Dancing Days" is dutifully centered on a riff that comes in at the start, but notice that it does not follow the usual Page formula. The notes aren't taken from a blues scale, there is very little melodic movement (the line doesn't jump around much), and there is a drone-like layer on which the riff sits. And although there is still movement in the guitars during the verse, the foundation is based on chords, not single-note riffs. Although Zeppelin certainly wrote in this style previously ("Your Time Is Gonna Come," "Thank You," etc.), what makes it notable here is that we are now into the second side of *Houses of the Holy* and have yet to hear a crushingly iconic Jimmy Page riff. According to Plant, "Dancing days are here again," and they bring with them a shift in songwriting sensibilities. For a closer look into "Dancing Days," see below.

To their credit, Zeppelin jumped on the reggae bandwagon with "D'yer Mak'er" at least a year before Eric Clapton released his version of Bob Marley's "I Shot the Sherriff." To their discredit, Zeppelin's concept of reggae is poor. Similar to the funk treatment they gave "The Crunge," Zeppelin plays heavy where the real practitioners of the genre keep it light. Page, Jones, and Bonham sound like they are attempting to perform a dexterous procedure while wearing oven mitts on both hands and the result is predictably clumsy. There's certainly no harm in the band having some fun in the Jamaican sun, but that doesn't mean it deserves to be on an album when solid tracks like "The Rover" or "Walter's Walk" were recorded but discarded. Regardless, "D'yer Mak'er" sold enough singles to make the American top twenty in 1973 and has remained a classic-rock radio hit so the song has many fans. Give it a listen and decide for yourself, but for comparative perspective take the time to hear Marley's *Exodus* as well.

Although John Paul Jones played keyboards on the first four Zeppelin albums, the instrument was usually limited to introductions or a support role. It isn't until "No Quarter" that we hear a true keyboard-based composition. This is at least partly due to new technology (and enough money to pay for it) that allowed both Jones and Page to build recording studios in their respective homes. Instead of having to book time at a recording studio in order to capture works-in-progress, Jones could track new ideas without having to take off his bedroom slippers. Page had used his studio to create a complete rendition of "The Rain Song" and Jones did the same with "No Quarter." This song makes for an excellent middle ground between the old and new Zeppelin. The verses are based essentially on chords (especially on two wonderfully dissonant choices heard for the first time at 0:48 and 0:54), but there is an old-school riff at 1:02 that reminds us of favorite Zeppelin moments. Although Page is prominently heard throughout "No Quarter," the recording is obviously driven by Jones and that's not a bad thing. For a closer look at "No Quarter," see below.

Jones is also primarily responsible for the songwriting foundation of "The Ocean" but it's as if "No Quarter" never happened. He is back on the electric bass and there are no moody keyboards getting in the way. This is blistering Zeppelin doing what they do best as a quartet: deliver good-time, riff-based rock and roll to make your head bob, feet tap, and hips sway. Zeppelin makes it clear on *Houses of the Holy* that they have some new ideas about where they want to go as a band, but "The Ocean" is a nice "thank you for listening" gesture. They know what their ocean of fans like, and they are happy to admit they like it too. For a closer look at "The Ocean," see below.

A CLOSER LOOK

"Dancing Days"

The interval of the devil returns to the music of Led Zeppelin, but instead of the sinister wail of "Immigrant Song," in "Dancing Days" the effect is pure exoticism. Indeed, Plant and Page were inspired by their travels to Bombay, India when writing the song for *Houses of the Holy*. The basic rhythm of the recording doesn't relate to any specific dance but it is rumored that the members of the band danced among themselves in post-recording jubilance. Zeppelin would push even further into exotic references with "Kashmir" and "In the Evening" on their next album, but "Dancing Days" retained a simple essence lost to those others: it's still just a cool rocking song. The lads remembered that rock and roll should be fun now and again, even when using peculiar harmonies from anywhere "over there."

"Dancing Days" wastes no time by opening up directly with the main riff of the song. The first notes we hear form the "flatted fifth" interval that historically caused great consternation for proper church composers when used in such an unapologetic manner. Page slides above and below the offending interval but its presence is keenly felt and suggests music of a far-off pagan land. But to keep the tune grounded, Jones plays a conventional bass pattern using hard-edged notes of the blues scale. Throw in the solid rock beat of Bonham and you hear a successful blend of the exotic and the well-trodden.

Plant begins his vocals at 0:17 with "Dancing days are here again; the summer evenings grow" and the most notable aspect is his complete lack of melody. He simply intones the same pitch throughout the entire phrase as if he is setting a chant tone for meditation. Moving ahead to the next phrase he refuses to budge off that note. A peculiar outcome is that by his not moving, Plant actually creates tension and release against the chords as they move underneath him. For his second complete phrase, "I got my flower" is completely stable but when Jones and Plant move the chord up slightly on "I got my power" a dissonance is created. However, the calm is quickly resolved by the chord moving back to the home position when Plant sings, "I got a woman who knows." His melodies are usually active and inventive but in this case Plant's nonmelody performs the task of supporting the exotic flavor of the introduction while still fulfilling the role of sonic trouble maker.

At 0:35 we hear a chord progression that moves in a slightly downhill direction and Plant deviates from his chant tone for the first time with "I said it's alright; you know it's alright; I guess it's all in my heart" followed by "You'll be only, my one and only; is that the way it should start?" This serves as a rare component in the bulk of Zeppelin's canon: a clearly defined chorus that follows a clearly defined verse. Jumping ahead to Page's work after Zeppelin, he eventually embraced the concept of an obvious vocal chorus (listen to his radio-friendly singles from the Firm with Paul Rogers or his album with David Coverdale for many examples), but throughout the 1970s he aggressively avoided it.

So it is with slight surprise we hear at 0:50 the beginning of another verse-chorus with the words "Crazy ways are evident in the way you're wearing your clothes." The only musical variation is the addition of an upwardly moving guitar figure at 0:56 that offers a countermelody to the inert singing of Plant. Page cleverly ties the verse into the chorus by carrying the same figure over into the following measures of music. This not only allows Page the opportunity to apply his guitar-as-orchestra skills, but it also provides useful variety to the otherwise-repetitive vocal chorus that offers nothing new.

By the time we hear the return of the opening "flatted fifth" material at 1:24 used as a transition to another verse, it might occur to you that there is one element found throughout Zeppelin albums that "Dancing Days" is missing: dynamics. The introduction, two verses, two choruses, and now the transition are all played with the same intensity and volume. As you listen to the remainder of the song you will not hear any substantial dynamic changes. A Zeppelin apologist might suggest that the mono-volume approach supports the Bombay-influenced exoticism and meditative quality of Plant's melody. The live version of "Dancing Days" from *How the West Was One* shows no attempt to alter the use of dynamics so perhaps the band was perfectly content with their choice. But taking a tougher approach, I feel the band got complacent in their songwriting and should have worked through a few more rewrites before committing the song to tape. The main riff is excellent and lyrics like "I saw a lion; he was standing alone with a tadpole in a jar" are good fun but without any ups or downs the song has no climax. It is hard to appreciate the light when there is no shade.

John Paul Jones makes an interesting contribution at 1:39 with one of the first appearances of a synthesizer melody on a Zeppelin album. Similar to his playing on "The Crunge," Jones uses the synthesizer on "Dancing Days" to approximate the role of a horn section. This figure replaces Page's guitar melody heard during the second verse and chorus. Although there is no effect on the overall volume of the track, this shows how Page (assisted by Jones in this case) was seeking multiple ways to provide each occurrence of the verse a unique identity.

A fourth verse-chorus set begins at 2:12 with Plant cherry-picking lyrics from earlier verses. A telling moment at the end of this chorus is that he offers an answer to the question "You'll be my only, my one and only; is that the way it should start?" In a surprising twist he emphatically states, "I know it isn't," ending on the same flatted-fifth pitch that nicely sets up the return of the main riff. Beginning at 3:00 we hear the only section of new music since the end of the first chorus. Although the guitar is the most dominant instrument here, these twelve seconds of music function as an "interlude" because the playing has more in common with preconceived orchestration rather than seemingly spontaneous improvisation.

After the interlude, we hear a last appearance of the flatted-fifth material at 3:13 and by this point it is apparent that the main riff is the

most interesting component of "Dancing Days." Unlike so many Zeppelin songs that are an embarrassment of riches with at least two or three
convincingly strong riffs or sections, "Dancing Days" goes all in with
one great idea and hopes you'll still enjoy the ride. It should be noted
that Plant felt no compunction to inject his vocals into the main riff. He
was content to take a lesson often demonstrated by his mate Bonham
that sometimes doing less is the best contribution to the whole.

"No Quarter"

Zeppelin fans went two albums without a Viking warrior reference since
"Immigrant Song" on *Led Zeppelin III* but the wait was worth it. The
brooding and keyboard-driven "No Quarter" from *Houses of the Holy*
was unlike anything in the Zeppelin catalog to this point and signaled a
shift that would stay with them. Beginning with "No Quarter," the band
created several lengthy, slightly dark, and sophisticated compositions
that featured lyrics with historical if not mystical themes.

When the song was originally recorded in 1972 it was performed a
half step higher in pitch than what ended up on the album. Page decided to slow down the speed of the tape, resulting in the lower key
than he thought would provide a murkier attitude. Interestingly
enough, "No Quarter" became a staple of Zeppelin's live set until their
final 1979 tour in Europe but they always played it in the pre-altered
higher key of D minor. This key allows for a much easier maneuverabil-
ity between the white and black notes on a keyboard and no doubt
Jones preferred it. When Zeppelin played their reunion concert in
2007, "No Quarter" was performed a half step lower than on *Houses of
the Holy* (resulting in C minor), meaning it was a whole step lower than
their 1970s concerts. This transposition facilitated Plant's fifty-nine-
year-old voice but in the video Jones can be seen playing the notes of D
minor just like he had all the times before. Rather than learn the song in
the lower key and losing the familiarities he liked, Jones made use of
the "transpose" feature on his digital keyboard. In this way, he could
press the notes for the key he preferred to play, even though the pitches
being heard are reassigned for Plant's benefit. All this shifting and
transposing over the decades has caused consternation for keyboardists
trying to play along with the recordings, but Jones has always stuck with

one pitch area and let technology move it as needed by vocalists and producers.

The first few seconds of "No Quarter" fade in as if we are walking into a room with the performance already underway. Jones begins the song unaccompanied on his keyboard and because the notes being played are from the minor scale, the music takes on a darker tonality. Zeppelin did not shy away from using minor keys (for example, "Since I've Been Loving You," "Tea for One," and "All of My Love") but they were careful not to diminish its impact through overuse and "No Quarter" stands out as the only minor-key song on *Houses of the Holy*.

A low bass note is heard at 0:16 reminiscent of a deep, droning bell but this is not Jones playing the note on a keyboard or overdubbing it later on the electric bass. Instead, he played foot pedals that were connected to a synthesizer, allowing him to perform bass notes independently of his hands on a keyboard. He had learned to use his feet years earlier as an organist but the synthesizer pedals would allow him a wider selection of sounds to trigger.

The solo performance of Jones continues until 0:48 when both Bonham and Page join in on a deliciously dissonant chord. For the next few measures Jones adds a few flourishes on the bass pedals but it is at 1:02 that a classic Zeppelin riff begins with Page and Jones joining together. If you listen through ear buds, the guitar and bass are panned to opposite sides of the stereo spectrum and you can hear the distortion and power coming equally from both of the instruments. Jones is again given a moment of solo playing at 1:30 and at this point we have now been introduced to all of the material to be used in the song: the brooding verse, the two dissonant chords used as a transition, and the epic riff. This is an unusual choice for Zeppelin to play through the entire form of a song before the vocals enter and it is no wonder that the total track time comes in at seven minutes. It is typical to hear an entire chorus of a blues or jazz standard played instrumentally, but to do it in this context reveals Zeppelin's willingness to patiently unveil the song. "No Quarter" is a prime example of a genre that rose out of the early 1970s called AOR (album-oriented rock) that eschewed any concern for traditional radio airplay and having a hit single. Zeppelin was continuing the charge in their movement to create artistic albums meant to be listened to in entirety as opposed to handing over radio-friendly chunks to a profit-minded record company.

When we hear Plant's first lyric at 1:46, it sounds as if we are right there in the room with him. The singer is using a very soft voice while standing close to a microphone and this creates an exceptionally intimate setting as he warns us to "Close the door; put out the light." Given the tone set by Jones on the keyboard, Plant's words are ominous and immediately draw you into the narrative. He conjures images of a weather-bound Norse cabin under imminent danger from an unseen foe with the words "Snow falls hard and don't you know; the winds of Thor are blowing cold." To enhance the eeriness, Page adds an echo that trails off the word *cold*. Plant really pours on the hero mythology when he sings, "They're wearing steel that's bright and true; they carry news that must get through" and the angst is supported by the music as Page and Bonzo return with the transitional dissonant chords. This tension is only partially relieved at 2:30 by Plant telling us, "They choose the paths where no one goes," and the band moves into the main riff. This is music and words that would be perfectly at home in a Tolkien rock opera (if there were such a thing).

As the riff repeats four times, Plant moans through the lyrical hook of the song by informing us that "they hold no quarter." Although it's not clear exactly who "they" are, we can assume they are some badass warriors who are not going to offer any mercy if they come across your path. Plant has done an impeccable job of matching his lyrics to the vibe of the music. By the time the second vocal verse begins at 3:00 we already have an image in our minds of Vikings, foul weather, shiny weapons, and secret messages that will save the day when delivered at the end of a perilous journey through desolate lands. Plant is writing excellent lyrics to have packed that all into just eight short sentences.

The lyrics are so compelling that it is almost disturbing when we do not immediately hear another verse to move the action forward but we are instead given another treat. Jones had not presented a lengthy keyboard solo since "You Shook Me" on *Led Zeppelin* but that absence is remedied beginning at 3:10 on "No Quarter" when he adds an acoustic piano track atop the electric piano. Although Jones would eventually expand this solo section to ten minutes or more when performing live, here he contains himself to only about fifty seconds, but there is much to be gleaned from the result. The opening piano passages are stacks of chords rather than soloistic single notes and this shows Jones's jazz influences. Pianists like George Shearing and Horace Silver developed this style of playing referred to as "chord-block voicings" but Jones seems to be emulating the classic performance of Bill Evans on the Miles Davis recording "So What." Featured on the iconic *Kind of Blue* album, Evans played the same type of block chords as Jones presents in "No Quarter" and to further the correlation, both songs were recorded in the same D minor key. If Jones was only going to have about a minute of soloing, he wasted no time telegraphing a coded message to jazz pianists everywhere that he listens to the right records.

At about 3:50, Page eases in with his own solo that is stunning in its mood and tonality. Here is a guitarist who made his reputation on blues-based rock and yet this solo exceeds well beyond those tenets. Page makes use of the blues scale as always, but he also exhibits what is called "modal" improvisation that just so happens to be a primary feature of the *Kind of Blue* album previously mentioned. This approach allows for the use of tones not found in the blues scale and provides an artist with many more colors on the palette.

To add even more sonic flavor, Jones adds some swirling and swooping synthesizer effects to the background of Page's solo but something quite unique is heard between 4:43 and 4:45. Do you hear the upwardly sweeping sine wave that seems to echo? This is called a Shepard's Scale (named for Roger Shepard in the mid-1960s) and is a rather complex auditory illusion in which a tone appears to continually ascend or descend and yet ultimately never gets higher or lower. This effect is readily available in the digital age but harder to come by in the still-analog year of 1972 so Zeppelin (likely Page) must have put considerable effort into creating/procuring a Shepard's Scale for "No Quarter."

With two high-caliber solos now concluded, Plant returns at 4:51 with a status update on our heroic marauders: "Walking side by side with death, [the] devil mocks their every step." These dark references are enhanced by a return to the keyboard-only accompaniment and the intimate nature of Plant singing directly into a nearby microphone using a quiet but desperately sincere timbre. We are reminded once more how "They carry news that must get through" but this time the follow-up lyric is different when Plant sings, "to build a dream for me and you." With the positive news that our warriors seem to have our backs, the band grinds once more into the main riff at 5:34 and never relinquishes it as they (especially Plant) jam their way to a slow fade that ends seven minutes after "No Quarter" began.

With the disparate styles found on *Houses of the Holy*, it was unclear in early 1973 which direction Zeppelin was likely to move in the years that would follow. The funk of "The Crunge" or (heaven help us) the reggae of "D'Yer Mak'er" were all possibilities, but it was "No Quarter" that ultimately foreshadowed their directional bent and the quality of Page's and Jones's solos reveal this preference. While "Dancing Days" was lacking in a caretaker's tender love, "No Quarter" was overflowing.

"The Ocean"

For the finale of *Houses of the Holy* Led Zeppelin buries a song worthy of being in lead-off position. "The Ocean" is riff-based in the tradition of "Black Dog" and "Good Times, Bad Times." These three rockers all share main riffs that take at least two measures of music to be delivered and they also have Jones as the originator. In the case of "The Ocean," Bonham is surprisingly given top songwriting credits followed by Jones, Page, and Plant. This is one of the rare Zeppelin songs to cite all the members as composers but the rhythmic twist found in the tune makes it appropriate to acknowledge the drummer, as well as the spoken intro.

As soon as you begin "The Ocean" you hear Bonzo in his gruff Midlands accent counting off the song in poetic fashion, "We've done four already but now we're steady and they went 1, 2, 3, 4," just before the band comes crashing in. It's tempting to guess Bonham is referring to beginning a fifth attempt at recording "The Ocean" but more likely he is only citing the four previous Zeppelin albums.

The primary riff of "The Ocean" has a funky signature that is due to two components. First, the pitches of the riff include both the minor third (near the beginning) to give it a blues edge and the major third (near the end) to create a brighter, soulful quality. Including both forms of the third is not unusual in the history of rock music but it is difficult to do in a way that does not hearken to boogie-woogie or rockabilly. Jones has a record of creating riffs that mingle notes from both the minor and major scales but "The Ocean" demonstrates a singular deftness. Second, the band cleverly drops half of a beat at the tail end of the riff but unless you are trying to dance along, this rhythmic skip sounds perfectly natural. Clap along with a steady pulse when the riff first begins and you will notice that your hands don't come together at the moment the riff starts over again at 0:13. This use of mixed meters was used sparingly in "Black Dog" but in "The Ocean" is a featured component repeated throughout the track and is another excellent example of Zeppelin's ability to play "loosely tight." When the band Rush repeatedly drops a beat during the synthesizer melody in "Tom Sawyer" or Yes drops two beats at the end of the lyric "mountains come out of the sky and they stand there" in their epic "Roundabout," we sense a studied self-awareness from the players that telegraphs their compositional deviation. But when Zeppelin plays "The Ocean," the rhythmic hiccup blows right by as if they forgot all about it. This is more akin to Big Mama Thornton dropping beats left and right in her pre-Elvis rendition of "Hound Dog" than the classically inspired peradventures of progressive-rock bands.

The opening riff continues for the first thirty seconds of the track before the vocals enter and we can learn a lot about the quality of Page's production skills from this portion. After all the others have recorded their parts and gone off to the pub, Page stays behind applying his years of experience as an audiophile. For one thing, there is an incredible brightness to all the instruments on "The Ocean." The guitar shimmers so much there are times you can hear inadvertent harmonics coming off the strings that falsely suggest Page is playing a harmony guitar part. And then there is Bonham's snare drum that crackles with life as he plays yet another of his groove-infused patterns. You might also notice that the squeaky drum pedal is back, but unlike the sparse "Since I've Been Loving You," it is thankfully less audible in the punchier "Ocean."

When Plant enters firmly at 0:30 with "Singing in the sunshine, laughing in the rain, hitting on the moonshine, rocking in the grain" he is creating an outdoor landscape with several elements of nature. However, a problem arises with the next couplet, "Got no time to pack my bag; my foot's outside the door; I got a date; I can't be late for the high hopes hailla ball." Those last four words are found printed in the liner notes for the album although they don't match syllabically with the audio. There has been much speculation over the years as to what the lyrics really are (a reference to Robert Johnson's "Hellhound on My Trail" is a leading contender) but Plant has not offered any conclusive answer and he doesn't sing with revelatory clarity on the available live versions. It wouldn't be the first time a singer simply jumbles up words during an otherwise excellent take so it stays on the album. Then during live performances the fumbled lyrics are retained to mimic the well-known recording or perhaps as nothing more than tongue-in-cheek humor.

The music shifted to a new pattern of chord strikes when the vocals enter but as soon as Plant wraps up his inarticulate "hailla ball," the band drops the main riff back in for four rounds with only intermittent vocal interjections of "ah-huh" and "oh, oh yeah." In other words, the primarily instrumental riff functions as the chorus of the song free of any vocal commitment. Consider for a moment the old Black Sabbath hit "Ironman." One of the most memorable riffs in hard rock begins in that track at 0:30 and then the vocals enter soon after. When Ozzy Osbourne sings, "Has he lost his mind; can he see or is he blind?" the best he comes up with for a melody is to simply double exactly what Tony Iommi is playing on guitar. Now return your attention to 0:50 in "The Ocean" and try to imagine how dreadful it would sound if Plant were to have used the Ozzy solution of singing along note-for-note with Page's guitar. Rather than forcing lyrics onto the best part of the song, Plant (and Page) knew the more satisfying choice was to sit back and let the groove breath on its own.

It's the second verse beginning at 1:11 where Plant gets down to sharing what the song is really about by using some not too veiled symbolism. With the words "Singing to an ocean, I can hear the ocean's roar," Plant is describing being on stage and looking out over a massive crowd that calls out for more.

The third "chorus" enters at 1:33 but this time Page plays over the main riff with a full-blown guitar solo. And unlike some of his solos that feature obvious organizational structure, on "The Ocean" Page just jams in the guitar-friendly key of A. Only when the band arrives at the next verse section (1:53) does Page convert from his free-form improvisation to an orchestrated use of chords. Since Plant was willing to step aside during the main riff, Page now responds by giving up what could have been more feature solo and replaces it with an ensemble-based interlude. Page was thinking about what makes the entire band sound better rather than merely proliferating his reputation as a gifted soloist.

To take things to an even more extreme level of minimalism, the band stops playing altogether at 2:13 and lets Plant take over. Using nothing but the syllable *la* Plant sings through four repetitions of a friendly sing-along melody tailor made for motivating his ocean of fans to join in. To add a little fun, Plant adds a pleasant harmony on the second time through and then on the fourth another harmony on top of that. This delightful doo-wop vocal break is enough to make us feel like the song comes not only gift wrapped but with a curly ribbon as well. These stacked harmonies seldom appear in Zeppelin music because they learned the hard way on their first album that allowing Page and Jones to sing background parts was not a good idea (listen to the ends of "Communication Breakdown" and "Your Time Is Gonna Come" for examples). When the "la-la" section of "The Ocean" was performed live Bonham would provide one of the harmony parts or Jones and Page would play them on their instruments. Of course, any omissions were easily overlooked as fifty thousand fans sang along.

Plant joyfully returns with a final verse at 2:37 to tell us that he used to sing to mountains before they washed away and he found a new object for his affections. The lyric "Now I'm singing all my songs to the girl who won my heart; she is only three years old and it's a real fine way to start" doesn't require much analysis to deduce Plant is singing about his young daughter. When the band performed "The Ocean" live over the next couple years, Plant revised the number to reflect her birthdays. After this verse we hear one more sweep through the main riff while Plant's vocal interjections become more energetic until he delivers us to the surprising last act of a song already rife with surprise.

With no warning, the band launches into a swinging dance groove with a triplet subdivision right out of 1958. Page leads the way playing his best Cliff Gallup (the guitarist with Gene Vincent) stylings while Plant drops in a smattering of doo-whop harmonies and Bonham chops away like Gene Krupa laying it down for the lindy-hoppers. After five albums and all the trappings that go along with being international rock stars, it's nice to hear that the four lads can still have a ripping good time. And Plant concurs as he ends the song with "Ah, it's so good."

6

TWICE AS NICE

Led Zeppelin's double album, *Physical Graffiti* (released in 1975), marks the band's arrival in their "epic" period as songs eight to eleven minutes in length beset all four sides. Keyboards gained dominance in a move to appease Jones (rumored to be leaving the band) and pervasive guitar riffs proved optional, making way for greater atmosphere and more of Bonham's groove. Having recorded more songs than would fit on one LP record but not quite enough for a full-length double album, the band decided to clear out the vaults and add tracks that had been cast aside from earlier projects. (This outtake-raiding would later explain the lack of post-breakup material, since few complete recordings were left unreleased.) The album became a smashing success and fans relished having "four sides" of new material for their growing Zeppelin catalog. "Custard Pie" and "Night Flight" are throwbacks to the band's hard-rock style, but with songs like "In My Time of Dying," "In the Light," and the droning "Kashmir," fans hear the power of Led Zeppelin in full flower.

Zeppelin kicks down the door without knocking when "Custard Pie" begins side 1 of *Physical Graffiti*. Except for "Grace" from U2 you won't hear a better disguised blues progression than the down-and-dirty "Custard Pie." And not since "Communication Breakdown" on *Led Zeppelin* did Jimmy Page craft a riff both easy enough to learn and awesome that most any teenager with a guitar and dream could plug in and play along. From the clavichord keyboard to the gravel in Plant's voice, "Custard Pie" is pure rock and roll. And we like it. For a closer look into "Custard Pie," see below.

"The Rover" was composed during the *Houses of the Holy* sessions but found its way onto *Physical Graffiti* instead. As good as Bonham's drum playing is, it's hard to imagine how the tune was passed over in the first place. In the guitar-friendly key of E, "The Rover" grinds along as Plant sings us through another variation on his favored topic of questing: "I've been to London, seen seven wonders; I know to trip is just to fall." And later: "In fields of plenty, when heaven sent me, I saw the kings who rule them all." "The Rover" has never gotten much attention despite being placed as the second selection on one of Zeppelin's most popular albums. The band didn't go out of their way to hype the song and except for a sound check caught on a bootleg recording, Zeppelin never performed "The Rover" as a complete track in a live performance. Too bad, as it would have been fun to see the look on Jones's face as he has nothing to do but redundantly pluck away at the same note during the jam at the end of the song.

At the 2012 Kennedy Center Honors, actor Ray Romano told the audience, "I lost my virginity to the first two minutes of 'Stairway to Heaven' . . . and I apologized for the next eleven; that's a *long* song." Romano exaggerated by several minutes (unless he played the extended live version during his memorable event) but he got lots of laughs because we assume Zeppelin couldn't possibly have played songs longer than "Stairway." But it's "In My Time of Dying" that is the lengthiest studio recording Zeppelin ever released. The track lasts 11:05 although the last fifteen seconds is actually just some studio chatter that reveals Zeppelin didn't really have an ending prepared. They sort of just stop playing on the same beat, and yet the fiery power of the previous eleven minutes is what remains brazened in your mind. If our ears are to be believed, the track was performed live in the studio all the way through and Page may have inserted a segment or two but there is only one guitar heard at any one time. Considering the length of the tune, this "live" performance is an absolute marvel for Led Zeppelin in the studio. Elements of "In My Time of Dying" (slide guitar and some of the lyrics) date back to gospel recordings from the 1920s but Zeppelin crushed it on *Physical Graffiti* and now symbolically owns the song.

The song "Houses of the Holy" was written and recorded for the album *Houses of the Holy* but inexplicably omitted. Why they passed over a song good enough to warrant being a title track but made room to include the sophomoric "D'Yer Mak'r" must make an interesting story to hear Page explain over a pint. The use of cowbell is a fresh choice for Zeppelin but maybe the band was sick of yet another track in which Bonham's foot pedal is heard squeaking. Plant's lyric speaks to young lovers going out for the night and in what makes a mantra for youth everywhere he asks, "Let the music be your master; will you heed the master's call?" Despite Plant using "houses of the holy" as a metaphor for concert halls, the band never got around to performing the song live.

In 1936, Robert Johnson recorded "Terraplane Blues" in which he uses elements of a car as a metaphor for a relationship. Plant took the idea even further into sexual references and found the perfect place to string them together over a clavichord keyboard riff Jones had been working on for a while. The song became "Trampled Underfoot" with a litany of not-so-subtle double entendre like "Dig that heavy metal underneath your hood; baby I could work all night; believe I've got the perfect tools" and there's also "Factory air-conditioned, heat begins to rise; guaranteed to run for hours, mama it's a perfect size." Plant often leans toward keeping his lyrics obscure or at least open to interpretation, but on "Trampled Underfoot" he unapologetically aims lower and easily hits his target. Jones hasn't created a riff as funky and cool as Stevie Wonder's "Superstition" but it's a strong entry in the Zeppelin catalog and gives him one more opportunity to show off his keyboard skills (and foot-pedal prowess).

"Kashmir" is one of the most identifiable Zeppelin songs on the planet. Even people who know little about the band can associate the main riff with the name "Led Zeppelin." "Kashmir" was used in its original form in the movie *Fast Times at Ridgemont High* but received even more attention for cinematic use after being altered. In the wild frontier of early rap music where the rules of sampling were still murky, Schooly D created a loop based on the "Kashmir" riff for his 1988 *Smoke Some Kill* album. If it had only stayed on the album, Page may have let it slide but when the track was prominently featured in the film *Bad Lieutenant*, lawsuits were filed and won. Existing copies of the movie were destroyed and the song was removed from future releases. In an ironic twist, Page later collaborated with Puff Daddy to use the "Kashmir" riff in a track connected to the 1998 movie *Godzilla*. Page had no problems with his work being adapted to rap; he just wanted to be paid and have a say in the quality control. Zeppelin considers "Kashmir" one of their highest achievements and they will proudly protect their baby from uninvited interlopers. For a closer look at "Kashmir," see below.

"In the Light" is an excellent example of what Jones was able to produce in the recording studio using his synthesizer. His lead playing during the introduction is as good as anything Pink Floyd offers in "Shine On You Crazy Diamond" and that says a lot. And Page's use of a bow on the acoustic guitar is an eerie delight. Unfortunately, the very aspect that makes the first 1:40 so good was the song's downfall when it came to live performance. Synthesizers of the era were very temperamental and could not be trusted to play in tune so Jones opted to keep the song off the stage. By the time technology had improved, the band was no longer together. "In the Light" is one more shining moment in the Zeppelin catalog and fully represents the band's love of long-form composition. The main riff doesn't begin for three minutes but it's one of Zeppelin's best and worth the wait. It slithers down a passage of notes that have no place in a hard-rock song, but Zeppelin (Jones) found a way. Be sure to listen for the descending bass line that first appears at 4:25 and how it moves in perfect counterpoint to the ascending figure from Page's guitar. Page eventually performed "In the Light" with the Black Crowes and the result is pure gold, not so much because of the performers' strong showing, but because of the song's innate power.

"Bron-Yr-Aur" is, as the name implies, a hold-out from the 1970 songwriting retreat Page and Plant took in the Welsh countryside. It's a short (only 2:06) but contemplative instrumental that fades in as if we've entered an inn where a fireside storytelling has just begun. Page's Martin guitar has never sounded more alive, like each note is ringing crystal. "Bron-Yr-Aur" marks the final appearance of an acoustic guitar feature on a Zeppelin album and sadly, a longer version of the song was never released on an official live recording.

"Down by the Seaside" is a sharp turn away from Zeppelin's trajectory in the mid-1970s. They were dogmatic in their efforts to appear free of influence by their contemporary rock giants. Comparisons to the Who, the Rolling Stones, or even the defunct Beatles were quickly ignored as nothing more than journalists inciting rivalry where none existed. And yet, here comes "Down by the Seaside," which might just as well be heard on a Stones or Neil Young record. The association may have been too obvious when the song was recorded (and rejected) for *Led Zeppelin IV* but a few years later Zeppelin was looking down from a mountain all their own and felt a good song deserved to be heard. For a closer look at "Down by the Seaside," see below.

On an album rich with epic songs like "In My Time of Dying," "Kashmir," and "In the Light," it's hard to believe there could be room for another. But room must be made for "Ten Years Gone" as one more grand pinnacle of Zeppelin songwriting and Page orchestration. At 3:20 Plant allows us to infringe on a private conversation when he sings, "Do you ever remember me baby; did it feel so good? 'Cause it was just the first time, and you knew you would." He hangs on the last word using a note that simply does not fit in the chord but the discordance is just what the lyric calls for and Plant boldly forces the point. Such moments combined with the riffs and chords within "Ten Years" scream for cine-matic use. Close your eyes and drift away with imagery of your own creation while listening to the sweeping layers of guitars (perhaps four-teen overdubs), classically inspired chord progressions, and Plant's lyr-ics of lost love and the choices of youth. Among the other gems of *Physical Graffiti*, "Ten Years Gone" is nearly pushed aside, but on any other Zeppelin album this would be a triumph of art and sound produc-tion.

On "Night Flight," take the time to focus on the drums. Here is a keen example of a rock drummer "playing the tune" the same way a good jazz drummer does in a big band. Remove all tracks but the drums and a Zeppelin fan can tell you what song it is because of the many fills and shifts in rhythmic patterns Bonham employs. The chords are only moderately interesting, there are no trademark riffs, and Plant's lyrics are too ambiguous to provide the song unique character. That leaves Bonham as the most interesting musician to listen to on "Night Flight" and he steps up nicely. This is a competent but unremarkable song and it's easy to see why it was left off of *Led Zeppelin IV*. "Night Flight" does no harm to *Physical Graffiti* but neither does it add any particular value.

The rock quartet is back, loud and proud on "The Wanton Song." No keyboards, strings, or wall of acoustic guitars getting in the way. The song is based not so much on a riff as it is a throbbing rhythm that bounces between octaves of the same pitch (akin to "Immigrant Song" but without as much forward-tilting swagger). Page uses the same reverse echo on his guitar at 1:23 that he pioneered on *Led Zeppelin* despite being told at the time it couldn't be done. In "Wanton Song," Plant gives a clinic on how to write a song about sex without pandering to the usual clichés: "Silent woman in the night you came, took my seed from my shaking frame, same old fire, another flame." And in case we grow concerned that our rakish Plant is becoming whipped to one wanton woman, he closes the song with "Feel my fire needs a brand new flame, and the wheels roll on." If not for "Custard Pie," "The Wanton Song" would have made an excellent lead for side 1 of *Physical Graffiti*.

In one of the very few Zeppelin tracks to feature an outside musician, pianist and Rolling Stones tour manager Ian Stewart adds a barrelhouse piano to "Boogie with Stu." The "Stu" is in reference to Stewart's nickname as he adds rollicking albeit slightly out-of-tune fun to this clap-along romp. The percussive rhythm of Bonham is as organic as they come and sounds like every pot, pan, and spoon in the kitchen is hand-slapped into submission. Plant borrows enough of the lyrics from Ritchie Valen's "Ooh, My Head" that a sixth-position songwriting credit is given to his mother (after the band members and Stewart). She sued them anyway. "Boogie with Stu" is the kind of music Zeppelin improvised spontaneously at concerts but doesn't hold up particularly strong on its own. Over the course of all their albums, Zeppelin incredibly has very few "filler" tracks and this sets them far above the output of their contemporaries, but "Boogie" isn't anything more than a studio jam with the tape deck rolling. With the gift of hindsight, "Boogie" offers nothing special to *Physical Graffiti* but would have been an excellent "outtake" had it been released for the first time decades later.

There is no bass on "Black Country Woman" so Bonham makes up for it by hitting his kick drum twice as hard. Fortunately, he oiled his foot pedal for this one. The basic track was recorded outside and Page didn't mind letting us know it by allowing a passing airplane to be left in the mix during the introduction. Except for the much slower "Tea for One" on *Presence*, "Black Country Woman" is the last song on a Zeppelin album derived from a blues progression. The genre had served the band well throughout their origins, but they were moving in new directions. "Black Country" is a final comment from Zeppelin as a folk-blues group and Bonham tries to arrive at the end a little quicker by pushing the tempo initially set by Page. Bonzo wins this one.

"Sick Again" sounds like it could have been written a few years later for the *In Through the Out Door* sessions. The song fits better in the vein of their late 1970s sound that is progressive in texture but simple in form. We hear a basic verse-chorus structure with a guitar solo in the middle just like every "hair" band in the 1980s would construct their MTV hits. And predating "Seventeen" by Winger or "Cherry Pie" from Warrant, Plant fires his lyrics straight between the eyes of the common rock-star conundrum in which the cute girl-groupies get younger while the band gets older. From behind the window of a Los Angeles limousine Plant sees pretty blue eyes and sings, "One day soon you're gonna reach sixteen, painted lady in the city of lies." Commenting on the plight of the girls with designs on cornering their favorite rock stars, Plant adds, "Clutching pages from your teenage dream in the lobby of the Hotel Paradise." If we take his words literally, Plant is admitting that it's hard to say no to young love: "The fun of coming, oh the pain in leaving, baby dry those silver eyes." Another shot of penicillin will keep him from getting sick again.

A CLOSER LOOK

"Custard Pie"

Zeppelin had proven regularly before the release of *Physical Graffiti* that they were masters at reengineering a blues progression into something distinctly "Zeppelin" while not totally abandoning the familiar. For example, "Since I've Been Loving You" is brimming with chords not typically used in a twelve-bar blues pattern and yet a casual listener will still correctly identify the song as derivative of the blues genre. The same can be argued for "Moby Dick," "Rock and Roll," and "When the Levee Breaks." But not so with "Custard Pie," which is one of the most well-disguised blues progressions to be heard in hard rock. And it's not that Zeppelin took extraordinary efforts to cloak the genre, but the cumulative effect of the rhythm, interesting chords, and vocal choices simply wipes out any breadcrumb trail leading us back to the blues. We are too distracted by the infectious riff, Plant's vocal timbre, and a ripping guitar solo to bother analyzing something as pedantic as song structure, but when the time is taken to break it down, the twelve-bar pattern is right there in front of us.

The beginning moments of "Custard Pie" lay down a gauntlet that challenges guitar players to this day. Page is slapping us across the face with a reminder that simple is a good thing. The opening riff is easy to play, easy to hear, easy to sing along with, and encourages seductive dance moves in either sex. That's rock and roll folks, and Page once again found a way to encapsulate it into only four beats. Clapton is the standard bearer for authentic blues lineage. Iommi owns the darker side of metal. Beck's sense of melody long ago surpassed his contemporaries. But Page is the master of consistently creating short, iconic riffs full of swagger and bullocks that will be played as long as rock music endures in any corner of the universe.

As Page fires off the first four rounds of his opening riff, Jones adds a little mayhem with a clavichord fill. The clavichord often shows up in songs that reference the occult, like Stevie Wonder's "Superstition" or the demon sequence in Charlie Daniel's "The Devil Went Down to Georgia" and Jones creates the same sense of dread in "Custard Pie." The instrument has been used to create some of the world's greatest music since the sixteenth century, but right or wrong, the clavichord is the tool for the rock keyboardist to announce that "something evil is going on."

After only eleven seconds, Plant enters with the words "Drop down baby; let your daddy see; drop down mama; just dream of me." This line is the same as heard in the song "Drop Down Mama" recorded by Sleepy John Estes in 1935 and illustrates another example of Plant's penchant for borrowing old blues lyrics. And for those few who recognized the lift, this is the first clue we might be hearing a blues-based song. The lyrics to "Custard Pie" are reasonably appealing, but the more striking element is the harshness of Plant's voice. His vocal cords sound like the result of being doused in gasoline just before inhaling a lit match. Although Plant has always had a rough element to his voice, the sound on much of *Physical Graffiti*, especially "Custard Pie," is far more guttural and shredded. This style of singing couldn't have been part of a long-term plan for vocal health and, indeed, years later Plant admitted to having surgery in 1975 to correct a problem. So while we might be impressed to hear Plant sing "Custard Pie" like he's been up all night having a whiskey-soaked yelling match, this is not the voice he would continue using. That may have played a part in the omission of the song in Zeppelin's live set despite its popularity. Instead, it was vocalist Chris Robinson who faced the comparison when he performed the song with Page as a member of the Black Crowes.

While Plant abrasively sings, "My mama allow me to fool around all night long," the chords begin to move at 0:21 as they would be expected to in the fifth bar of a blues progression but there are two ways Zeppelin obscures the action. First, the distinctive use of syncopation as the band steps their way downward until returning to the "home" riff distracts us from assuming Zeppelin is just pacing through another mundane take on the blues by a British rock band. Second, Plant contributes to the subterfuge by not repeating the opening line during these measures, which would have been the conventional choice in a pure blues progression.

The chord moves again at 0:32 to exactly what would be found in a blues progression and Zeppelin once again muddy up the harmonic waters by adding three more chord hits before getting back home for the last measures of the main riff. If you take the time to count, you will arrive at twelve measures for each sequence of the form but the nonrepetitive nature of Plant's lyrics and the clever use of syncopated chord inserts mislead us into thinking a more modern structure is being applied. And it works in Zeppelin's favor that we can be easily distracted by the cool factor of the main riff that appears three times during each pass through the form.

Beginning at 0:42 we hear the first of two more stanzas and quite uncharacteristically, Page doesn't throw in some little ear candy to differentiate the latter verses. This means we are left to listen to the vocals for fresh content but Plant makes this difficult due to the rasp in his voice and unclear enunciation. At the very least we can detect the bluster of Plant as he warns his conquest to throw her man out the door because he "ain't no stranger" and has "been this way before."

Before the third verse is officially over Page breaks protocol by launching his guitar solo but with only twelve measures available in each pattern he carved out a little extra time by not waiting. Beginning at 1:42, you will notice Page plays in a very emotive, almost "speaking" tone and this is accomplished through the use of a wha-wha pedal. As Page plays notes on his guitar, he engages the pedal and a filter manipulates the signal based on the pedal's position. This is akin to a trumpet or trombone player affecting the sound of their horn by closing and opening a mute in the bell of the instrument. Unlike Page's subdued "ensemble" solo in the middle of "Down by the Seaside," this time he claims hierarchy in the audio mix and the guitar is clearly the dominant instrument for all fourteen measures.

When the solo concludes at 2:17, Plant enthusiastically returns with a verse and gives us the song title. Although he's not easy to understand, the words are "Your custard pie yeah, sweet and nice; when you cut it mama, save me a slice." At this point, Plant succumbs to the magnetism of the blues and he repeats the same lyric in a traditional manner until the twelve measures are completed. From about 2:45 onward "Custard Pie" opens up into a lengthy jam over the main riff and Plant even whips out the harmonica to supplement his vocal improvisation. At 2:53 Plant grinds into a vocal phrase that he feels is important enough to repeat three more times and there is guarded agreement that he sings, "I'd sure like a piece of your custard pie," but your guess is as good as the next one. With many of Plant's lyrics, it's less about the path and more about the journey.

"Kashmir"

The first and lasting appeal of "Kashmir" is the pounding riff based on a cycle of three-hit chords. Even die-hard Zeppelin fans don't hold themselves accountable to know enough lyrics to sing along with "Kashmir" because that's just not the point. This is a song to enjoy viscerally in your gut with a sense of wanderlust. Your eyes close and you are transported to a harsh desert land and lost tribal caravans. And when you finally do take the time to learn the lyrics they are all the more brilliant in their vivid imagery and poetic sophistication. "Kashmir" is the stand-out track on *Physical Graffiti*, one of Zeppelin's greatest recorded achievements, and a radio mainstay despite its playtime of eight and a half minutes. Radio program directors learned the lesson since "Stairway to Heaven" that conventional time restraints were not to be placed on Zeppelin. To further prove the song's permanence in the rock pantheon, "Kashmir" has shown itself to be adaptable to classical or-chestration, choral arrangements, and even hip hop treatments. Al-though there have been many songs since 1975 that are obvious descendants of "Kashmir," there was really no precedent beforehand from the Zeppelin catalog or anywhere else for that matter. It sounded new, and exotic, and empowering, and Zeppelin nailed it.

"Kashmir" was not cooked up last-minute in the recording studio to fill out an album short on material. This song marinated slowly between 1973 and 1975 taking on layers of more complex flavors along the way. Page crafted the main riff as part of an ongoing guitar cycle from which he would sometimes pillage thematic ideas. Only much later did Jones contribute his string parts played on a Mellotron keyboard, which led to the eventual addition of an orchestra. In Cameron Crowe's notes to *Led Zeppelin: The Complete Recordings*, Plant shared how the origins of his lyrical contribution to "Kashmir" came from a drive through North Africa:

> The whole inspiration came from the fact that the road went on and on and on. It was a single-track road which neatly cut through the desert. Two miles to the East and West were ridges of sand rock. It basically looked like you were driving down a channel, this dilapidated road, and there was seemingly no end to it. "Oh, let the sun beat down upon my face, stars to fill my dreams. . . ." It's one of my favorites.

"Kashmir" explodes in the opening second with a Bonham cymbal crash emphasizing the moment. The three-hit sequence begins with each succession slowly ascending in pitch until reaching an apex after three measures and beginning again. With Bonham playing a pattern based on four-beat measures, the two patterns come into alignment at the end of every third measure, which is out of keeping with the tendency in pop music to base most sections on chunks of four or eight measures. This tertiary grouping places a burden on Plant to resolve his melodic phrases in less time than he is used to.

We hear two cycles of the main riff before Plant enters at 0:18 with the aforementioned "Oh let the sun beat down upon my face, stars to fill my dream." He digs into the word *stars* in his idiomatic manner in which the letter *r* gets extra attention, a trademark any vocalist in a Led Zeppelin tribute band acquires. Plant continues to create his desolate setting with "I am a traveler of both time and space to be where I have been." And in the classic tale in which the protagonist journeys to seek knowledge from far-off lands, Plant tells us he meets elders who "talk of days for which they sit and wait when all to be revealed." His last note trails off while holding a dissonant note (called the ninth of a chord) that adds to the exotic Eastern flavor permeating the music.

While Plant sustains the word *revealed*, an orchestra of strings and brass enters. Over the years, Zeppelin had only ever allowed a few musicians outside of their quartet to appear on record (percussionist Viram Jasani on "Black Mountainside," vocalist Sandy Denny on "Battle of Evermore," and pianist Ian Stewart on "Rock and Roll" and "Boogie with Stu"). So it notable that on "Kashmir" the band sought not just an outside guest, but an entire orchestra. Using skills from his pre-Zeppelin session days, Jones arranged the music that begins at 0:54 in which the orchestra plays a descending melody offering balance to the ascending nature of the primary riff. The additional musicians greatly enhance the depth of the recording and their absence was a problem when Zeppelin performed "Kashmir" live in the 1970s with only the limited keyboard/synthesizers of the day.

Listen carefully to the orchestra music between 0:54 and 1:05 for two oddities. First, you will notice that when the descending line begins, the ascending main riff continues underneath and the two parts clash. While it's possible this is an intentional "counterpoint," it is likely the main riff was already mixed to tape in a way that could not be removed. This is supported by the fact that when Zeppelin played "Kashmir" in concert there was never an attempt to have the two parts present at the same time. Second, when the orchestral descending line ends at 1:05, there is a ponderous seven seconds where nothing much happens. This is another example of how the main riff, based in groups of three, didn't match up to the rhythm of the orchestra figure so we have to wait out the discrepancy. This would also explain Bonham's seemingly errant cymbal crash at 1:03 that lines up with the primary riff rather than the secondary. Cymbal crashes usually announce an arrival point, but in this case Bonham rolls out the red carpet and no one comes in.

For the second verse there is a new string figure added at the end of each cycle of the main riff to add variety around Plant's vocals. But, as a response to the odd number of measures involved, Plant quickly runs out of things say in this verse and resorts to the fail-safe "Whoa-oh, whoa-oh" before the orchestra moves ahead to the secondary riff at 1:48. This portion includes yet another wayward Bonham cymbal and a few leftover beats to meander through until repeating the secondary riff one more time at 2:06 but this time driving toward something new. And just to keep things interesting, Zeppelin purposefully drops half of a beat during the transition figure at 2:11. Tap your foot along with the slow pulse moving through this section and you'll quickly get dislodged unless you accommodate for the meter shift.

Arriving at 2:13 we hear the third riff of the song that is still based on the same key (D in this case) but Page and company add contrast by playing less and letting Bonham's incessant groove propel the momentum. The drums are wonderfully audible throughout this section and not a squeak is heard from the foot pedal. The new riff is based on a two-measure pattern but Page and Jones are out of the way at the beginning of the second measure leaving Bonham with several unaccompanied beats. Choosing not to overexploit the opportunity, Bonham plays in lockstep so that the kick drum matches up precisely with the guitars and then he adds only small dashes of style in the open space. Here is one of the most powerful drummers ever to play in a rock band being perfectly content to lay down the law not with wild abandon but with a perfectly wicked drum beat. Plant adds to the open use of space with sparing interjections of "Mama, there ain't no denying" and "Ooh, I've been crying" using his guttural, rock-god wails. Lasting almost one minute, Zeppelin unapologetically takes their time with this section. It doesn't develop in any substantial way but makes an excellent soundtrack during a late-night trek down a dark desert highway.

Next, there is a brief return of the second riff but it is only transition material toward the fourth main component of "Kashmir." Beginning at 3:22, we hear two new chords, each one lasting two measures. Unlike the syncopated punchiness of the third section, the rhythm section now plays with a contented smoothness that offers a pleasing contrast. This point of relaxation leaves room for Plant to deliver more lyrics and demonstrate his flair for melody. He conjures up scenes of windblown desolation when all he sees "turns to brown as the sun burns the ground and my eyes fill with sand." And in keeping with his pursuit of knowledge, he adds, "Trying to find where I've been" with the last note hanging on a high pitch that holds through to the return of the main riff at 4:19. In this way, Plant's voice is the bridge between the side adventure of the two-chord jam and the return to the larger quest to be found on the original road.

The third verse begins at 4:38 and we have now heard all the compositional elements found in "Kashmir" even though the band plays on for nearly four more minutes. The music now offers only repetition, but it doesn't stop Plant from delivering what may be the best lyrics he has ever written. He first shares a traveler's prayer with the words "Oh pilot of the storm who leaves no trace like thoughts inside a dream; heed the path that led me to that place; yellow desert stream." Then, in what is the only direct reference to the song title, Plant swears an oath: "My Shangri-La beneath the summer moon, I will return again; sure as the dust that floats high in June, when moving through Kashmir." And finally, returning to a prayer, he pleads, "Oh father of the four winds fill my sails across the sea of years; with no provision but an open face, along the straits of fear." Heady stuff for a long-haired kid from West Bromwich, England.

The band grooves onward to find their way back to another two-chord jam at 6:36 where Plant soars above both the sinewy orchestra lines and monstrous Bonham drum fills (with an interesting chorus effect on his drums). The last thirty seconds feature a slow fade that, like the entire song, takes its time. Many other artists have covered "Kashmir" but are seldom as brash as Led Zeppelin when it comes to length of delivery. Violinist Lucia Micarelli keeps her orchestra-accompanied rendition under five minutes. Vocalist Ofra Haza clocks in her version at five minutes. When Puff Daddy reimagined the "Kashmir" riff into "Come with Me" for the *Godzilla* movie soundtrack in 1998, he only kept at it for about six minutes. The all-girl Zeppelin tribute band Zepparella keeps theirs to about 7:45. Only Heart, who has played several Zeppelin songs with loving care over the decades, gave "Kashmir" its full run of well over eight minutes when they toured with Jason Bonham in 2013. Borrowing nothing from the many less-patient artists who have adopted the song, Zeppelin played a version lasting about 8:45 at their 2007 reunion concert, proving that even decades after giving life to "Kashmir" it is still the best when presented by its birth parents.

"Down by the Seaside"

Physical Graffiti is bursting with powerful riff-rockers like "Custard Pie," "Trampled Underfoot," "Kashmir," and "In the Evening," so it is all the more delightful when a pleasant gem like "Down by the Seaside" is able to hold its own in the presence of such iconic beasts. Page and Plant composed "Seaside" back in 1970 during their songwriting se-questration at the Bron-Yr-Aur cottage and then recorded it during the sessions for *Led Zeppelin IV*. At that time the result didn't make the cut and remained in the vaults until space opened up on the double album of 1975. "Seaside" offers a counterbalance to the heaviness found on many of the other *Physical Graffiti* tracks and is as close as Zeppelin gets to sounding like a mellow Neil Young or sauntering Rolling Stones. There is no account of Zeppelin ever performing the song live but Plant revisited "Seaside" when he recorded a version with Tori Amos in 1995. He and Amos treated the remake like it was grisly bad medicine, far unlike the friendly sing-along manner of the original.

"Seaside" kicks off with a jaunty drum fill just before the band en-ters. Page's guitar is dripping in watery vibrato and void of any distor-tion. Jones uses his bell-like electric piano and bass foot pedals that allow him to record both parts during the same take. And Bonham sets the mellow mood with a light shuffle in no hurry to get anywhere.

Plant and Page wonderfully match the tone of the music to the lyric. From the opening phrase Plant intones his wish upon us to take a moment to reflect on our lives and the world around us: "Down by the seaside, see the boats go sailing; can the people hear what the little fish are saying?" The music rolls along unobtrusively until Plant laments at 1:04 that "the people turned away" from his well-meaning advice. Keep in mind that the lyric writer is a twenty-two-year-old self-identifying hippie who feels bad when he sees "all the folk go racing" with "no time left to pass the time of day." Spending hours in the countryside with his mate Jimmy must have made Plant all the more in tune to how he saw humanity turning away from the simple pleasures of life. Of course, Plant didn't mention the fact that his rock-star excesses in the world of commerce and technology were the very reason he was able to afford time communing with nature.

Jones must have loved busting out an old Floyd Cramer (famous for his classic country song "Last Date") piano riff for the break at 1:11. Getting the most out of the time he spent learning the figure, he plays it a second time at 4:12. It was widely speculated that Jones was tired of touring in Led Zeppelin during the time leading up to the *Physical Graffiti* sessions and was strongly considering leaving the band. He took some time off before returning to the studio and deciding to stay on. It's easy to imagine Jones hearing the playback to a song like "Seaside" at the moment of his Cramer-esque riff and thinking, "This ain't so bad."

After two passes through the form of the song, an interesting shift occurs at 2:08 where the band casts off their outside influences and sounds decidedly like Zeppelin. Bonham leads the way by fluidly transitioning out of the lazy country shuffle into a straight rock beat. This in itself is only moderately notable but Zeppelin makes it harder for themselves by simultaneously speeding up the tempo. It was on "Stairway to Heaven" that the band expertly employed the same device and this may have been part of the reason "Seaside" was left off of *Led Zeppelin IV*. Hearing the same trick twice on one album would have lessened the impact of either song. The increase in tempo on "Seaside" is from about 95 beats per minute up to 105, which is enough to be perceived as an increase in energy without being jarring.

For the new section, the change in tempo is matched with a shift in harmony from the carefree brightness of C major to the menacing melancholy of A minor. The latter just sounds more rock and roll and Page digs in immediately with a funky rhythm at 2:13 followed quickly by a solo at 2:18. But differing from his all-dominating solos like those heard in "You Shook Me" or "Stairway to Heaven," on "Seaside" Page keeps the volume subdued so that the lead guitar is part of the tapestry. Page maintains equal sonic interest in the underlying groove and the sustained vocal backgrounds and the result is an ensemble texture rather than a soloist and his accompaniment. This portion of "Seaside" is awash with layers and you have the option of focusing in on one instrument at a time, as if you were studying only a portion of a larger painting, or standing back and letting the complete picture settle in.

The jam comes to a close at 2:48 when Plant asks, "Do you still do the twist?" He seems to be informing us the 1960 dance is a lost secret of youth that only the enlightened few take advantage of when he adds, "I wanna tell you, some go twistin' every day though sometimes it's awful hard to tell." And on the word *tell* the rhythm and tempo shift with no preparation back to the original feel for a repeat of the song's introduction. Such an abrupt adjustment can be a clumsy affair but Zeppelin shows complete confidence in the maneuver. The effect is that whatever troubled waters we were on have run their course and we are returned to the easy current and soft, bayside breeze.

The band casually drifts through another two verses with no variation from the earlier appearances. Only Plant provides any variety by offering up some final thoughts on how we might yet become attuned with our great maker: "Sing loud for the sunshine, pray hard for the rain, and show your love for Lady Nature and she will come back again." Youthful optimism expressed through overly simplified hippie lyrics in a pleasant and understated song: just what Zeppelin fans need now and then to reconcile having our minds blown asunder by the likes of "Kashmir" and "Custard Pie."

7

FEELING THE PRESENCE

Led Zeppelin reached the height of their musical prowess—and popularity—in the mid-1970s. No band was bigger. But their future came into serious question after Robert Plant's near-fatal car accident in 1975. Rather than waste time during recuperation, Page and Plant met in Malibu, California, to try writing some new songs. Sensing excitement in the results, they called Jones and Bonham to rehearse and record their seventh studio album, eventually titled *Presence*. All of these tracks are stripped-down rockers with not an acoustic guitar or keyboard to be heard. The album provides good-time grooves found in "Candy Store Rock" and "Royal Orleans" but also delivers one of their most epic journeys with the ephemeral "Achilles Last Stand." After the diversity of *Physical Graffiti*, critics found the one-dimensional sonic punch of *Presence* lacking, and the album proved one of Zeppelin's slowest sellers. Even the band seemed unsure what to do with songs from *Presence* when they added only two of them to their later set lists. Hardcore fans, however, often find more than enough satisfaction with the band's return to simple production values, cryptic but catchy lyrics, and unfaltering rhythmic drive.

"Achilles Last Stand" is the opening track on *Presence* and fulfills the promise made with "Kashmir" and "In the Light" from *Physical Graffiti*. Zeppelin might still indulge with simplicities like "Boogie with Stu," but the band was at their best with long-form rockers and loud multi-layered guitars. "Achilles" is the powerhouse crown jewel of *Presence* and equally as thunderous when the band performed it live, which they did many times. It's a shame Zeppelin didn't find a way to include "Achilles" in their 2007 reunion concert but it's waiting to be played and enjoyed whenever we want. For a closer look at "Achilles Last Stand," see below.

"For Your Life" wins the award for best use of tambourine on any Zeppelin track. The extra bit of percussion is as close as *Presence* gets to having flowery orchestration. The easygoing pace combined with the hard-edged guitars and vocals make this one heck of a good rock song. Contemporaneous bands like Black Sabbath and Deep Purple were more facile at breakneck tempos, but no one like Zeppelin could get so much feeling out of a relaxed tempo. Slower grooves run the risk of exposing weaknesses but Zeppelin never minds the challenge. Most of the credit goes to Bonham: the heaviest-hitting drummer in the pack. For a closer look at "For Your Life," see below.

If "The Crunge" was Zeppelin's attempt at going outside the box to play a funk song, "Royal Orleans" was the result of bringing what they learned back to their own house. "Orleans" is not a funk song, but it's not wrong to call it funky. From the very beginning, listen to Bonham make his drum beat suggest a forward-moving shuffle, even though he's not playing a shuffle beat. He is the master of presenting a simple beat and then adding just enough personality to create the illusion that there's more going on. Listen especially for the moment at 1:06 where Bonham strikes his open hi-hat three times in quick succession, which beautifully hands off the same pattern to Plant when he sings, "Naa, naa, naa," a few seconds later. Plant's lyric is a semi-autobiographical tale about the band meeting up with some transvestites who came back to the Royal Orleans Hotel one night. Jones explains the rest in an interview from the December 2007 issue of *Mojo Magazine*:

> That I mistook a transvestite for a girl is rubbish; that happened in another country to somebody else. . . . Anyway "Stephanie" ended up in my room and we rolled a joint or two and I fell asleep and set fire to the hotel room, as you do, ha ha, and when I woke up it was full of firemen.

Transvestites, drugs, and firemen: just another day on tour with Led Zeppelin.

If you don't like the opening moments of "Nobody's Fault But Mine" you are in trouble because it takes up considerable time throughout the track. But there are many other aspects to like. The verse is classic medium-tempo Zeppelin laying down the law. The surprise harmonica feature reminds us that Plant is a fine soloist on the instrument and raises the issue that he should have played more often. The tone Jones is getting from his bass is huge and nicely complements Bonham. And Page picks up the gauntlet laid down by Plant to play a high-grade solo of his own. But that introduction . . . how it plods along.

"Candy Store Rock" is a throwback with a twist. The lyrics are in line with classic Rhythm and Blues double entendre where the surface meaning is clean enough for radio but everything sounds naughty if you want it to. Plant isn't going for subtlety when he tells his girl, "Oh baby baby, it ain't the wrapping that sells the goods; oh baby baby, I got a sweet tooth when my mouth is full of you." By the end of the song Plant has us convinced he is quite the candy connoisseur. The twist comes from how complex the rhythm gets even though the lyrics and general style suggest it's just a simple Elvis rocker from 1958. Every time you think you know where the first beat of the measure is, it's jumped away again. It's difficult to find a mid-tempo rocker from Zeppelin that hasn't been covered numerous times by bands, orchestras, string quartets, and glee choirs. But "Candy Story Rock" remains largely untouched. It's sweet to hear but daunting to play. Even Zeppelin never got around to it in concert.

The stutter-stops at the beginning of "Hots on for Nowhere" make for a great introduction. It's like a handle is being cranked a couple times before the engine turns over. And it's a pretty funky motor once it gets going. Whether Plant is singing about the heat of day or handing out a playful "La-la-la," this is one of his better melodies. It perfectly complements the guitar and bass without simply imitating them. Even if most of his lyrics are indiscernible, we get caught up in the infectious groove and sing along anyway. If anyone ever tells you Page doesn't impress as a soloist, play "Hots on for Nowhere" because he's in excellent form and it's a tune that hasn't gotten much traction. As Plant sings shortly before the end, "It feels so good."

If there were no "Since I've Been Loving You," the last song on *Presence* would be the finest slow blues Zeppelin ever recorded. "Tea for One" is drenched with anguish and dark thoughts. When Plant sings, "A minute feels like a lifetime when I feel this way," there is no hint of irony or clever metaphor. He means exactly what he says and it's a hellish place to be. Page outdoes himself as a soloist but don't ignore his work as a rhythm guitarist on "Tea for One." Every chord and riff is lovingly placed on the exact beat when it is needed to keep the pace slow and lamented. While "Since I've Been Loving You" moves steadily toward a grand climax, "Tea for One" remains a slow burn for over nine minutes right up until the final meandering chord. Be careful of your mood when you listen to this one because it will take you somewhere pensive and real.

A CLOSER LOOK

"Achilles Last Stand"

After the release of their previous two albums, Zeppelin now had a precedent to live up to. With "No Quarter" on *Houses of the Holy* and both "Kashmir" and "In the Evening" on *Physical Graffiti*, the band was expected to deliver an epic rocker on all future albums. They did not disappoint with the release of "Achilles Last Stand" on *Presence*. And similar to "Kashmir," there was scant precedent from any of their previous work for "Achilles." To the Zeppelin fan it appeared from the ether. The hammer-crushing rhythm of "Achilles" is reminiscent of "Immigrant Song" from *Led Zeppelin III* but that track barely got warmed up before it was over in less than two and a half minutes. Multisectional form was found in "Stairway to Heaven" and allowing a song to develop with molasses-drip patience was heard on "In My Time of Dying," but the sheer unyielding rhythmic drive and riveting guitar work lasting over ten minutes on "Achilles" was stunningly new. Zeppelin had never done anything like it before nor would they again. And even though it is unique in the band's catalog, "Achilles" has become a signature, or even stereotype, of their style. The song was a one-off achievement on *Presence* and yet somewhere along the way began to represent the ideal of what they must have been meaning to do all along. Jones, Plant, and Page often cite the song as one of their favorites and it came up as an inside joke when the three surviving members appeared on American television with David Letterman in December 2012. They were asked to describe their music and without missing a beat the normally reserved Jones cracked up the audience by playing air-bass and mimicking the rhythmic aggression of "Achilles." Jones was admitting on behalf of the band how they are fully aware of their reputation and willing to have some self-referential fun with it.

The unaccompanied guitar introduction sounds like chiming bells coming to you from across the hills, reverberating just beneath low-hanging clouds. There is menace in those rolling chords. With a thunder-crack of energy, the band attacks the first riff at 0:19 and won't release you from their clutches for the next ten minutes. Page has his overdubbed guitars coming through the speakers like his own personal army and Bonham is locked into the nuances of the rhythm with march-like precision. If all the guitars were removed, Bonham's drumming is so integrated we would still be able to identify the song hearing only him. Most hard-rock riffs, including those of Zeppelin, last one or two measures, but the opening riff of "Achilles" is four measures. And proving from the outset the band is in an epic mood, Plant does not approach the microphone until the lengthy riff has cycled through four times.

The lyrics Plant does finally provide at 0:45 immediately reference one of his favorite topics: journeying in a quest for knowledge. The opening line of "It was an April morning when they told us we should go" is followed by "As I turn to you, you smiled at me; how could we say no?" This use of (mostly) rhyming couplets with each line having a pause becomes the structure for the entire lyric and there is no deviation across the ten couplets that follow. Although he employs repetition here and there, usually on nonworded vowel sounds like "oh," there is nothing in "Achilles" that functions as a chorus. The lyrics are all exposition and development, and with a total of eleven couplets, this is one of Plant's wordiest lyrics.

At 1:12, there is an instrumental transition between lyrics but the riff does not change. The only difference is that during the two occurrences of the main riff, Page and company play with more intention and syncopation. These additions are dispensed with whenever Plant returns so that attention is readily focused on the lyrics. After telling us of glancing kisses and steaming streets, Plant closes out the second round of verses (and fourth couplet) with "Oh to sail away to sandy lands and other days; oh to touch the dream, hides inside and never seen." Once again, Plant has his protagonist off to unknown lands where mystery waits and answers loom. And showing some playfulness in the studio, Plant occasionally double-tracks the second half of each couplet, which broadens the sound and literally adds more weight to the delivery of the words.

Our ears are gifted something new at 1:52 when a new riff begins but it is short lived. This is another of those riffs worthy of being the anchor piece of an entire song but Zeppelin only trifles with it as a bit of flotsam. It's at 1:58 that they deliver the true secondary theme. The pounding rhythm that has thus far been relentless is now abated and replaced with a riff that climbs steadily for two measures, takes a brief moment to look around, and then climbs again for another two measures. This is a widely spaced staircase and Bonham accents each step with smashing cymbal crashes. During this ascension, we hear Page bring in a lead-guitar tone that is backed by a wall of sound and it is these moments that support the reputation of *Presence* as a *guitar* album in no need of keyboards or vocal harmonies. The climbing melody sustains into the return of the main riff (busy version) at 2:11, which nicely bridges the two ideas together.

Entering at 2:25, Plant picks up the tale of his wayfarers with "Into the sun the south, the north, at last the birds have flown" and later, "Oh to laugh aloud, dancing as we fought the crowd." During performances of "Stairway to Heaven," Plant was known to ask the audience, "Does anyone remember laughter?" Jovial delight among friends is another consistent theme in Plant's lyrics over the years as can be heard in "Achilles," "Stairway," "Misty Mountain Hop," and "Dancing Days" among others.

Notice how Page inserts compositional variety at 2:51 by adding a new guitar melody that brings a fresh dimension to the instrumental passage between Plant's vocals. Little by little, Page is adding more guitar as the song progresses. We've actually only heard three main components to the song so far (the introduction, the main riff, and the climbing theme), and Page adds material by adding layers in a vertical manner rather than expanding the song horizontally with completely new sections. In this way, our ears are not overwhelmed too early with a plethora of ideas, so by Page adding them gradually, we are able to retain the old and enjoy the new with equal clarity.

Even with the growing number of guitar parts, it is only at 3:43 that we hear Page break into an obvious solo. It occurs while the rhythm section (including Page's guitars added before the solo track) begins to rumble through four cycles of the climbing riff. Although Page's solo has an air of improvisation about it, he is seeking a strong melodic line that reveals the seriousness of the moment. He conveys "composing" rather than being mistaken for "jamming."

While the solo continues, we hear new accompaniment begin at 4:10. Shifting to a radically different tempo (tap your feet coming into this section and nothing matches up without adjustments being made), Bonham leads the charge with a blast of four machinegun hits played four times in a row followed by one beat of silence. Not only does Zeppelin pull off another tempo change as they did previously in "Stairway" and "Down by the Seaside," but here they also go one step further by shifting to a time signature with five beats in each measure, which is rare in classic rock ("Living in the Past" from Jethro Tull is the best example of an exception). If "Achilles" were to be used as film score music, this would be the scene where the hero cuts and slashes his way through the seemingly insurmountable enemy. As good as Page's solo is, we are also drawn to the rhythmic fierceness of the accompaniment and reminded that Zeppelin was a band of three highly skilled instrumentalists. Coming out of this five-beat attack at 4:22, we are only at the midpoint of Page's solo as the band plays through another four climbing riffs. Page finds notes on his guitar that portray a sense of unsatisfied yearning. We hear him searching but never ultimately arriving. And when the band comes around for another blast from the machinegun time change, this time they change it slightly by adding two more hits (played half as slow as the others) on the previously empty fifth beat. Even though it's only two extra notes, they create a momentum that drives us onward through the melee while Page continues his quest for the perfect melody.

Plant returns to us at 5:15 (the song is barely half over!) and ends his tenth couplet with "Oh the sweet refrain, soothes the soul and calms the pain; oh Albion remains, sleeping now to rise again." This is a slightly veiled reference to Arthurian legend. "Albion" is an ancient name for England often only used in classic poetry or literature. And as a loyal subject of the crown like Plant would know, "sleeping now to rise again" refers to the Knights of the Round Table who are portended to someday wake from long slumber and aid in England's return to past glory. It is notable that Achilles never actually makes an appearance in the lyrics of "Achilles Last Stand." Perhaps Plant was fond of the Achilles heel metaphor as a song title but preferred not to literally mesh Arthurian and Homeric themes in the same song.

In the last full couplet at 5:54, Plant sings, "Wandering and wandering, what place to rest the search; the mighty arms of Atlas, hold the heavens from the earth." Considering this last line is in the only lyric in the entire song that Plant repeats (at 6:15 and again at 8:58), it should be viewed as important. A specific meaning to Plant's words is in the eye of the beholder, but generally speaking, his protagonist seeks an end to the journey and perhaps it will be found in the mercurial infinite of the gods.

Meanwhile, Page continues to add more layering to his tour de force. Particularly notable is the funky exchange between Page and Plant beginning at 7:30. After exhausting all eleven couplets, Plant is out of lyrics and scat-sings a sexually charged "ah-ah-ah-ah" with a pouty uptick on the last note, but direct your attention to the lightning rhythm guitar work of Page. He demonstrates considerable restraint to have waited until the last charge of the main riff to release this funky and slightly evil pattern. Even though Plant contributed worthy lyrics throughout "Achilles," it now becomes clear it is Page who will push the epic journey through to the end by adding even more guitars than before. Notice there are now two solo parts calling and chasing each other at 8:25 and compare this to the earlier portions of the song where there was only one. Had he played both parts earlier, there would be nowhere left to go at the end and Page knows this so he patiently limits the energy and doles it out in controlled portions. And now at the song's closing moments we are surrounded by his army of six-stringed warriors.

Plant makes some final, mostly nonworded contributions to the sonic fray until the band collapses on itself at 9:45 where Page stands alone in the smoldering ruins to play the solo-guitar figure used nearly ten minutes earlier as the introduction. Take a moment to acknowledge the underheralded performance of Bonham and Jones, who hammer away for the bulk of the song, never getting a breather or the spotlight (especially Jones). With chime-like quality, Page announces the song's conclusion and we are left wondering the outcome of our hero's journey. Was there knowledge found and a glorious return? Or a funeral pyre for a tragic lost cause? It's this lack of certainty that maintains the Zeppelin mystique. The answers are not handed to us, but maybe we will move one step closer to enlightenment by playing the song just once more, and once more after that.

"For Your Life"

In their post-Zeppelin years, Page and Plant were more high profile than Jones and there were greater expectations placed on them to create music "as good as before." Faced with this unenviable task, they both struggled to find material that sounded like they had moved ahead and yet was still true to their past. As a member of the Firm with Paul Rogers (from Bad Company, who was also on the Swan Song label), Page came up with songs like "Midnight Moonlight" and "Satisfaction Guaranteed." They featured an earthy quality and swampy groove with a hint of dark uncertainty in the lyrics. Meanwhile, as a solo artist, Plant came up with "In the Mood" and "Big Log," which, while using a lighter touch of guitar in favor of synthesizers, essentially went for the same aesthetic as Page's Firm. Independently of each other, they were both trying to advance upon the very thing they had created earlier in "For Your Life" on *Presence*. "For Your Life" is not Zeppelin's lost gem or misunderstood, red-headed stepchild. But it is a strong indicator of what the band wanted to be doing in the coming years, even if they floundered about trying to complete the job without each other as co-conspirators. Interestingly, they didn't see enough value in "For Your Life" at the time of its release to include it in concerts, and the song was never performed live during the band's reign. But when Zeppelin re-united for a full-length performance in 2007 it was the surprise item on the set list and treated as if it were a new song. Time had proven the tune's worth as a harbinger of potential and the band forever elevated the status of "For Your Life" by admitting its relevance at such an important concert.

The opening seconds of "For Your Life" are contrasts in motion. The rhythm section jumps right in with syncopated hits displaying a hard-edged but relaxed (if not refrained) quality. And yet, lightly in the background is a spritely tambourine playing in double time. As Plant would sing decades later in "Down to the Sea" from *Fate of Nations*, "Life is a big tambourine; the more that you shake it the better it seems." Keep in mind while listening to "For Your Life" that no matter how much Page and Jones gently weep with their guitars, there is the happy tambourine offering an alternative to the gloom. Notice also in the instrumental introduction that Page does something he was often guilty of in concert but usually cleaned up for studio recordings. There are a few occasions where he hits an extra note that sounds unintended but, causing no harm to the chord of the moment, no correction was made. This cavalier "leave it in" attitude wouldn't work on their epic rockers, but for the mid-tempo, low-expectation "For Your Life," an extra note or two gives the song a dash of street credibility.

Plant's first lyric at 0:23 is "You said I was the only, with my lemon in your hand" and we are tossed right back to the citrus metaphor from "The Lemon Song" on *Led Zeppelin II*. On the 1969 album he sang, "Squeeze my lemon until the juice runs down my leg," so for him to bring it up again, it's nobody's fault but his that fans kept bringing the tart fruit to concerts. But Plant's initial playfulness dims as he sings about having to pull away from a woman to save himself. And in his only direct reference to hard drugs on any Zeppelin album, the woman asks him, "Don't you want it? Don't you want cocaine, cocaine, cocaine?" There isn't an autobiography of a 1970s rock star that doesn't admit cocaine was everywhere and that it seemed everybody was doing it. But to directly name the drug in a lyric was pushing it. Plant could claim innocence because it is an evil woman offering up the powder and he is just a victim of her wiles. It also helps when Plant contorts the lyrics throughout "For Your Life" enough that parents of teenage Zeppelin fans were able to convince themselves they heard nothing suspicious. And to further quash any drug-snorting accusations, Plant clears himself by adding, "Hadn't planned to, could not stand to try it." But of course we can see the wink in his eye and fingers crossed behind his back.

"For Your Love" is another Zeppelin song in which the members take their time between vocal segments. The result is an unhurried steadiness that creates suspense as we wonder how long the wait will be for more information about sex and drugs. Starting at 1:05, the band plays four rounds of the introductory riff with each one lasting two measures. For 20 seconds we hear Jones, Bonham, and Page playing as a tight, well-rehearsed rock band, but technically we've already heard this several times by now. Tunesmiths aiming for top-forty radio airplay live by the adage, "Don't bore us; get to the chorus," but such things do not factor into "For Your Love," which doesn't even have a proper chorus. This is music intended to be absorbed as part of an overall album, not digested as an individual morsel doled out on pop radio. It is this album-oriented philosophy that played a part in Zeppelin being one of the last major rock bands to release their catalog as digital downloads. They weren't able to reconcile how their albums would be purchased piecemeal and heard outside of their original context. Zeppelin eventually conceded to their younger fans who did not grow up in the age of the "album," but back in 1976 "For Your Love" was a classic "AOR" track.

The second verse begins at 1:26 and includes obvious cynicism compared to what we often hear from Plant. He sings, "Heard a cry for mercy in the city of the damned," followed soon by "Down in the pits you go no lower; the next stop's underground." With words about being damned in underground pits, Plant is in a far darker place than putting flowers in his hair on a trip to California. He offers the character in his song no clear path to redemption and the strain in his voice goes far to support the attitude. Keep in mind Plant is doing much of his singing for *Presence* while seated and healing from an automobile accident so it's not a leap to sense his frustration about the present and concern for the future (at one point during the session Plant fell and there was worry that he had done permanent damage to his still-broken leg).

The last lyric of the second verse marks a brilliant move by Plant to melodically propel us to the next section beginning at 2:07. He ends with, "You didn't plan it; you overran it" and holds out the last word on a high note that matches the harmonic "key" of the song, which is normally nothing unusual. The difference here is that the band has "modulated" to a higher key, which adds a sense of drama. Tension is created by Plant resolving to the note that should have worked but now sounds at odds because the band has jumped away to a new chord. Notice Plant's elegant solution is to slowly stretch his voice upward until joining Page and Jones. By the time Plant bends his way to the new key, our ears have slid along with him and feel entirely comfortable with the shift. Also notable here is the busier bass line funky enough to reveal the influence of James Jamerson and Donald "Duck" Dunn on Jones.

At 2:28 we hear a new section of music that functions as a bridge. Plant's tambourine is ever present but the rhythm put forth by Bonham is something special. The band already mixes things up by dropping two beats but Bonham takes it further by inverting the backbeat. In the most basic of rock drum patterns, the kick drum plays on the first and third beats while the snare drum is accented on the second and fourth. This has been a benchmark of rock music since Ike Turner, Chuck Berry, and Little Richard started playing. Since a snare drum is brighter than a kick drum, we hear the second and fourth beats as being louder and the resultant phenomena is called the "backbeat." By inverting this beat, Bonham swaps where the snare and kick drums are expected to be played and our ears are temporarily confused. The pulse is still strong and unmistakable but there is an uneasiness coming from the drums that feels as if things could tumble down. A classic use of the inverted backbeat is Cream's "Sunshine of Your Love" when Ginger Baker turned things around on the first two verses. This is the kind of trickery drummers know about (often because of Baker) and in "For Your Love" Bonham found his own place to drop it in. (For another good example of an inverted backbeat, listen to "Just What I Needed" by the Cars beginning at 2:12.) Meanwhile, we hear Plant sing the occasional "Do it when you wanna" in pleasant two-part harmony that gives the song a lightheartedness that is oddly out of sorts with the rest of his lyric.

Do not be deceived at 2:50 that we are hearing another introduction leading to the third verse. Although these measures are suspiciously similar to the earlier verses, that is not what Zeppelin is playing. Instead, they have taken the riff played at the modulation and shifted it to the original key center. Our ears are tricked into thinking that Page and Jones went "home" to the opening material but it is just an aural illusion. The giveaway is the busy bass line of Jones. And to make the structure of "For Your Life" all the more convoluted, Plant begins singing a melody that could be construed as a completely new version of a verse. With yet another obvious cocaine reference, he sings, "When you blow it babe, you got to blow it right" and, sounding positively exasperated, he adds, "When you fake it baby, you're fakin' it for your life." This is followed by another pseudo-chorus of "Do it when you wanna," which still doesn't make much sense lyrically but it serves as an adequate transition to an inspired Page guitar solo.

There is limited discussion in this book about specific guitars used by Page but it should be noted that he long favored using a Fender Telecaster in the recording studio while turning to the Gibson Les Paul for concerts. Of course there are many exceptions, but those were his two go-to choices. On "For Your Life" Page opted for neither and

instead played a blue Fender Stratocaster that he would make considerable use of as a member of the Firm. This is important because it
symbolizes Page's interest in revitalizing his sound while in Zeppelin
even if the development of that goal was ultimately delayed to later
projects. He was pushing himself as a soloist and his efforts are well
represented by the Stratocaster solo in "For Your Life."

The very fact that the guitar solo doesn't even begin until 4:17 is
more proof that Zeppelin was completely at ease with letting "For Your
Life" develop slowly. Page's first phrases through 4:30 often emphasize
darker or dissonant tones of the scale. Like "No Quarter" on *Houses of
the Holy*, his style of soloing is distancing himself from the blues in
favor of what is called "modal" improvisation. Although there is inciden-
tal movement in the accompaniment, it is essentially based on only one
chord for the duration of the solo, which allows Page ample time to
develop his musical story. Without the distraction of navigating changing harmonies, Page delivers his most cohesive solo of length on record.
The guitar tone and melodic choices demonstrate Page's willingness to
match the mood of Plant's lyrics. He is choosing to serve the needs of
the song, rather than using a song as a platform to support his ego as a
soloist.

Plant returns at 5:02 to say, "On the balance of a crystal, payin'
through the nose," which again has an overt coke-snorting connotation.
He is not shying away from announcing that someone has a nasty problem and it will come with a price. This line is sung over the music for
the verse that hasn't been heard for about three minutes. Our ears take
to it like a friend we didn't realize was missed. Plant's last new lyric for
the song comes in the form of a suggestion (if not a warning) for his
imbibing acquaintance: "And now your stage is empty, bring down the
curtain; baby please fold up your show." Speculation about copious
drug use within the Zeppelin camp has been common fodder for the
media over the decades, but if these lyrics are interpreted literally,
Plant is definitely taking sides and asking someone he knows to make a
change for the better if it isn't already too late. As he says twice as a final
caution at the song's end, it's "for your life."

8

TURN THE PAGE

Rumors always plagued Led Zeppelin about rampant drug abuse, especially by Jimmy Page. The most obvious sign of Page's disconnection to his usual attention to detail is on the 1979 album *In Through the Out Door*. Keyboards dominate many of the songs, along with production choices that would appear in the later solo work of both John Paul Jones and Robert Plant. For the group, the only way to move the album project ahead on a schedule, given Page's unpredictability, was to simply plow ahead without him. This often resulted in Plant and Jones spending time in the studio without the other members. Critics and fans split over the "new" sound. Some saw it as progressive and inevitable; others cast it as a betrayal of the band's hard and fast ways. Synthesizers permeate the album and on "All of My Love" even assume the solo position generally reserved for Page. That song also features the pop form of verse/chorus that Page had so adamantly avoided—further evidence of his reduced involvement. Jones and Plant, probably enthused by their increased position of power over the band's songwriting, looked forward to a tour that would share the new direction with the world. But rock-star debauchery finally caught up to John Bonham, who was found dead by Jones on September 25, 1980, after a night of binge drinking. The greatest rock band of the 1970s soon announced they could not continue without their original line-up. The album that was meant to serve as a transition to a more rounded and progressive sound became a final statement. While limited outtakes and concert recordings waited in the recording vault, *In Through the Out Door* became Led Zeppelin's swan song of newly recorded studio material.

The three-year wait was finally over with the beginning of "In the Evening." Zeppelin fans had never faced such a long period without the release of a new album and the first track on *In Through the Out Door* meets the qualifications of a good start. There is a mystic and moody introduction, ethereal lyrics delivered by Plant in healthy form, dominant drumming from Bonham, and a powerful riff that makes Page sound right at home. And at almost seven minutes in length, Zeppelin comes out of the gate full of confident vigor. For a closer look at "In the Evening," see below.

"South Bound Saurez" (a misspelling of the intended "Suarez") is an endurance test for Jones. Not since David White played "At the Hop" has a song asked a pianist to bang out the chords so many times for the length of the track. Jones's enthusiasm is infectious and motivates Bonham to deliver some stellar footwork on the kick drum. Page also gets caught up in the New Orleans–inspired groove but his solo is not a direct hit in the bull's eye. Another hour or two in the studio would have improved his contribution but Plant makes up for it with the extra vocal tracks singing the delightfully fun "Sha-la-la-la" in do-wop harmonies.

No one outside of the Zeppelin camp would ever have expected them to come up with a song like "Fool in the Rain." There was never little more than a whisper of Latin influence on any of their previous records and out of nowhere comes a fully formed and mature composition with all the trimmings. This is still unquestionably a Led Zeppelin song but the fusion of styles is a thing of beauty and far more successful than their wanderings toward funk ("The Crunge"), reggae ("D'yer Mak'r"), or country ("Hot Dog"). For a closer look into "Fool in the Rain," see below.

"Hot Dog" is a mess of a song. Plant has a great time riffing on pickup trucks, U-Haul trailers, and the general store, but the words themselves aren't country and Plant knows better. Page is an Olympian of rock guitar and a master of audio production so why he suddenly tosses his reputation into the back of this Texas-sized insult is anyone's guess. Many 1970s rock bands recorded these kinds of send-ups to blow off some stress in the studio, but it's another matter entirely to waste the listener's time by releasing a low-brow studio jam on a Zeppelin record where every groove is prime real estate.

"Carouselambra" is good enough to wash away all the sins of "Hot Dog" and then some. This is ten and a half minutes of glorious, inspiring, monumental songwriting and performance. In the grueling Tour de France bicycle race, the longest and most grueling day of the three-week event is referred to as the "queen stage." That is the perfect designation for "Carouselambra," and not just because of pure length. This is the kind of recording that serves as a turning point for all that came before and all that follows. Had Zeppelin stayed together into the 1980s, "Carouselambra," the queen-stage of *In Through the Out Door*, would have served as the musical compass for the next album and beyond. For a closer look at "Carouselambra," see below.

"All of My Love" is a well-crafted and creative pop song. But Zeppelin was never about pop songs, so it is confusing to hear such a thing on one of their albums. And, in what was a great disappointment to Page, the chorus, which does little more than repeat "all of my love," is pandering and simplistic. The chords are user-friendly and anticipate the kind of middle-of-the-road rock from REO Speedwagon and Journey that would soon engulf the airwaves. To Jones's credit, he enhances the recording with a brilliantly composed synthesizer solo that keyboardists have enjoyed playing since 1979. And how did the public react to this red-headed orphan that showed up on a Zeppelin album? It was an unqualified hit played on mainstream pop radio all over America. After a decade together, they finally had a popular record fit for general consumption. But compared to the band's previous "pretty" songs like "Babe I'm Gonna Leave You," "Thank You," and "That's the Way," there's something not quite satisfying about "All of My Love." For one, Page is practically absent from the track and his playing during the verse and chorus is entirely inconsequential. Can there really be a credible Zeppelin song in which Page's guitar is of no importance? With the release of "All of My Love," Plant and Jones voted "yes."

With an honorable nod of appreciation to the triplet-laced ballads of Wilson Picket and Otis Redding, Jones wraps up *In Through the Out Door* with the most gorgeous introduction he ever wrote for the band. On "I'm Gonna Crawl," the synthesizer technology of 1979 doesn't quite sound in tune as he mimics a string orchestra but in the light of such lovely notes, the shortcoming is forgiven. The three main chords of the verse unhurriedly saunter by as Plant croons to us: "'Cause she is my girl and she can never do wrong; if I dream too much at night, somebody please bring me down." Could it be that little Robert Anthony is finally in love? The drummer, for one, was duly impressed. According to Chris Welch in his *Led Zeppelin Dazed and Confused* book, Bonham considers "I'm Gonna Crawl" one of Plant's best vocal performances. At 3:20, Page reaches deep into his soul and finds a guitar solo worth crawling to hear.

A CLOSER LOOK

"In the Evening"

After waiting over three years for a new Led Zeppelin album, you rush home with your new purchase to hear for yourself what a few of your friends have already told you about. The first delightful moment is spent tearing through the brown paper wrapping that obscures the cover photograph used on your particular copy. Six different images of the same pub setting were used and until you paid for a copy, you didn't know which version of the cover would be yours. Then racing to put side 1 of the LP on your turntable, you set the needle in the groove, turn up the volume, and wait for "In the Evening" to begin.

The introduction to "Evening" fades in so slowly that you turn the volume up again in anticipation. Why is it taking so long? The sounds begin to take on recognizable form and you detect the low drone of a synthesizer, the ominous rolling of tympani drums with an added chorus effect, and a melody instrument that is haunting and slightly familiar in timbre. Where have you heard it before? Then it comes to you. It sounds like Jimmy Page is stroking a violin bow across the strings of his electric guitar like you saw him perform in the *Song Remains the Same* movie. Although technically Page is using a device called a Gizmotron, the end result is still a bowed guitar string. The use of a bow is so firmly associated with Page that no other guitarist can even consider the technique without an immediate (and most likely negative) comparison. As the introduction of "Evening" continues swirling, you are gravitationally pulled into Page's exclusive domain. This is a fusion of the classic (Page on guitar) and the new (Eastern influence and synthesizers) and the sound is enticing. All that is missing is Plant.

At 0:53 the singer delivers the song title in a simple, chant-like style that hands you the aural landscape to be imagined. With the phrase "in the evening," your mind fills in the blanks with whatever it is you associate with evening. For some, that means twilight, dim stars, cool air, the hush of the day's end, and peaceful pleasantries in good company. For others, it means loneliness, lamentation for the loss of another day wasted, turning to vices for comfort, pondering the great unknown, and longing for all that life has not delivered. Rather than force specifics onto your psyche, Plant makes use of vagaries that kindle the imagination with unlimited outcomes. As Plant sings the final syllable of *evening* you notice a brief sense of resolution as the low drone, Page's wandering guitar melody, and the vocal all converge on the same pitch. But as is often the case with Zeppelin music, the lack of tension is a temporary condition.

Blasting in at 0:58 is the first of three chords that define the song. Rather than a riff of individual notes ("Whole Lotta Love" or "Black Dog," for example), the cornerstone of "Evening" is the repeated playing of the same three chords spread over two measures. The chords themselves are not unusual and are used in many rock classics like "Sweet Home Alabama," "Takin' Care of Business," and "Can't You See." The originality comes from the power of the rhythm, especially with the third chord's entrance on a syncopated beat at the tail of the first measure. That chord then sustains through the second measure, leaving prime, unfettered real estate for the vocals of Plant.

Plant starts off telling us in first person about troubles with a lady: "When the day is done I'm looking for a woman, but the girl don't come." However, he abruptly abandons any hints of autobiography by shifting the bulk of the lyric to the second person. He assumes the role of an older brother and sings, "So don't let her play you for a fool; she don't show no pity baby; she don't make no rules." The rest of the lyrics can be interpreted as the dialogue between two individuals: one blindly in love, the other giving wizened counsel.

The "lover" of the two completely ignores the "brother" and calls out to his intended conquest, "Oh, oh, I need your love . . . I just got to have." This lyric begins at 1:35 and functions as a chorus but is such an overused and simplistic sentiment that it's possible Plant intended these words to only be used as a temporary placeholder. During the *In Through the Out Door* recording sessions, Zeppelin recorded the song "Ozone Baby," which uses only "Ooh, it's my love" as a chorus. Being nearly as trite as the chorus to "Evening," "Ozone" was dropped from the album and only released later on *Coda*. Vocalists often sing nonsensical or mundane lyrics early in the process of songwriting hoping that something more substantial will come to them later, but in the case of "Evening" the chorus was deemed sufficient.

The brother returns with mild chastisement at 2:11, telling his ward, "I hear you crying in the darkness; don't ask nobody's help," and then, "Ain't no pockets full of mercy baby, 'cause you can only blame yourself." This falls in line with a growing willingness for Plant to be more judgmental and introspective in his lyrics as he ages. We heard it in "For Your Life" and find it again in "Evening" as well as "Fool in the Rain" on *In Through the Out Door*.

The second chorus begins at 2:31 but your ears pick up something you hadn't noticed earlier. Since the words to the chorus are rather pedestrian, Plant is driven to find other ways to make the words interesting and he comes up with a peculiar solution. He elects to use such a unique pronunciation of *your* that you are temporarily misled by what sounds like "I need *Jew* love" but the context of the surrounding words clears up the confusion. It is standard vocal practice to alter vowel sounds in the higher registers to make them easier to sing ("ah" might be replaced with "ooh" for instance), but Plant is still in a comfortable vocal range and he already proved in the first chorus he could pronounce *your* correctly, so he is just having some fun making an otherwise unremarkable lyric more memorable.

The third verse begins at 2:50 and you hear Plant continue to offer advice but this time it takes on a self-referential vibe that could be applied to Plant and his bandmates. He shares how it's "lonely at the bottom, [but] man, it's dizzy at the top." This is a clever reversal of the cliché that preaches only the top is lonely. And then, as a bright-spot resolution, Plant tells you that "if you're standing in the middle, ain't no way you're gonna stop." Plant, who by this point has experienced both economic hardship and opulent excess, is suggesting to his pupil (and you, the listener) that the path to happiness is through focused moderation in all things. And moving ahead to the third chorus at 2:31 you can't help but want to know which version of the chorus Plant will sing for you this time. Once again, he finds the word *your* too obvious.

Many fans of Led Zeppelin are at the very least guitar enthusiasts and quite possibly players of the instrument. Even with the preponderance of keyboards on *Houses of the Holy, Physical Graffiti*, and *In Through the Out Door*, the guitar is still at all times present in a substantial role (the one exception being "All of My Love," where Page's contribution is worthy of a session player but expendable as a guitar god). Assuming you are a guitar-friendly Zeppelin fan, what you hear at 3:42 drops your jaw and will become one of your favorite Jimmy Page moments of anything he ever records. The beginning of his solo conjures visions of a caged Tasmanian Devil bursting free of a wooden enclosure sending splinters and shards in all directions. Page creates this sound by manipulating the springs of the whammy bar connected to the guitar bridge but the result is stunning and unlike anything he had ever recorded. Similar to a fanfare of trumpets announcing the presence of royalty, Page is warning all guitarist-interlopers who may have emerged in his three-year recording absence that he is still the man. The effect is repeated at 4:00 and is just as impressive. Page is criticized often (and accurately) for being disengaged on *In Through the Out Door* but this solo alone evens the score.

Since the main riff began at 0:58 you have heard no variation in dynamics. Zeppelin usually shifts the volume a few times in their better songs but in "Evening" they don't release the intensity until Page leads the guitar solo into a new section at 4:22. At first you feel like the band has slowed down but you can still tap your foot at the same tempo as before. To create the illusion, they are playing everything in "half time" in which the tempo does not slow but everything takes twice as long to play. This entire portion of the song lasts sixteen measures and you sense the relaxation being conveyed by all the musicians. Bonham backs off so much that he practically removes himself from the mix. Jones plays carefully constructed bass figures but with a light, unobtrusive touch. The diving and driving lines played on the synthesizer are replaced with pleasant sustained chords. And over it all, Page delicately sings a melody on his electric guitar. As is so often the case with great music that moves from loud to soft, you find yourself anticipating a rekindled charge of energy and Zeppelin obliges with a sustained and impassioned wail from Plant that leads the band back to the explosive main riff for the final verse.

Beginning at 4:57 you hear Plant impart the view that "whatever that your days may bring, no use hiding in a corner 'cause that won't change a thing." In the few years leading up to the recording of "Evening," Plant had endured the risk of throat surgery, a crippling car accident, and the death of his young son, so he might as well have been giving the kindly advice to himself as well as the forlorn love-seeker featured in the lyrics. During those dark days there was considerable speculation that Plant wasn't willing to continue as a member of Zeppelin but, just as he incorporates into his lyrics, he made the decision to forge a path beyond hiding in the corner.

Considering that you have heard four verses, the one thing missing from "Evening" that is commonly heard in the music of Zeppelin is added tracks that provide a unique identity and sense of development to each successive verse or chorus. For the first five and a half minutes of "Evening" each section of the song is a near duplicate of the previous version of that section. As gripping as the main riff is, the impact begins to wane after so much unaltered repetition. It is only in the fourth and final chorus that Zeppelin magnifies the accompaniment and, not surprisingly, it is Page doing the job with his guitar. He adds a climbing melodic figure at 5:33 that lasts two measures before being repeated. And as we've heard so often from Page, he likes to exploit his ideas as much as possible so at 5:43 when the chords shift up he shifts his new idea up the same interval and plays it two more times. This melodic line is strong enough that it's surprising he waited until the last moment to unfurl it.

You hear Plant finish up his last declaration of needing "Jew love" before the band fires off a final salvo of the main riff at 5:52. Page joins in with an added track of lead guitar at 6:02 and you are not surprised when you hear him repeat it again at 6:20. In between he shows off his whammy bar by striking a note and then dragging down its pitch before releasing the bar and allowing the upward return. Other rock guitarists, especially those in alignment with Eddie Van Halen in the years after Zeppelin's demise, make copious use of whammy-bar gymnastics but for Page it was a rare treat.

You begin to hear the music fade at 6:30 and it's tempting to set the needle back at the beginning and immediately hear the entire track again. The exotic introduction, the first airing of the main riff, Plant's quasi-autobiographical lyrics positioned as a conversation between two entities, a triumphant Page guitar solo, and the modern edginess of the keyboard parts brilliantly orchestrated and performed by Jones make "In the Evening" a fan favorite. Decades later the recording still stands tall and withstands the "dated" qualities reflected in so much music from the same era. Zeppelin did not pander to the times with drum machines (even though Jones was using one to assist in the songwriting process), disco beats, slap bass guitar, or girl background singers. Even though they were pushing ahead with synthesizers, copy-and-paste repetition, and whammy-bar guitar solos, "In the Evening" is still unwavering rock music played by rockers capable of embracing change without it defining them.

"Fool in the Rain"

Zeppelin wastes no time in "Fool in the Rain" by opening the song with the main riff. We determine within the first few measures that this is unlike any previous Zeppelin song. The riff is based purely on the major scale instead of the blues scale we often hear in rock music. This bright melodic sensation is supported by the buoyant beat Bonham plays on his drums, which floats along with a rhythmic snap. Furthermore, although we hear the piano, there is also an electric bass part so we know that Jones didn't cut corners by playing foot pedals. Even though Jones has decent performance skills on the foot-pedal bass, he is far superior when the low notes are played with his fingers on the four-stringed bass. Returning to the main riff, it is made up of two halves, each lasting two measures. The first half is comprised of six notes that move up the major scale with a seventh note that balances the score by dropping down a full octave. The second half features the exact same riff but without the seventh note. The last note of each half is the fifth pitch of the major scale: a note that is often used to set up an expectation of "going home" to the first note of the scale. This is a subtle way to manipulate us into waiting to hear the resolution, which comes with the first note of the next riff. But then the cycle begins again: the tension is set and then resolved repeatedly throughout "Fool" and if you feel drawn in, now you know why. The smooth rhythm heard in the introduction is deceptively simple and trained musicians can analyze it several ways. Suffice it to say there are "polyrhythms" created between the main riff and Bonham's shuffle-like pattern but all the parties intersect every time the riff begins anew. And if you suspect there is a distant compositional kinship between this riff and "La Bamba," you are correct.

Lyrically, "Fool" is built on the humorous theme of a lovesick man waiting on the corner for his girl and passing the time thinking about her with a growing sense of trepidation. At its heart, Plant has written a love song, which is not commonly found on Zeppelin albums. Plant often sings of love but only in "Fool" does he develop an obvious, first-person account of pursuing a relationship and the crestfallen outcome. Only on this, Zeppelin's eighth album, does Plant allow himself the simple pleasure of telling a sweet tale of courtship without feeling the need to couch it in Tolkien mythology, Homeric journeys, or mystic introspections.

With greeting-card romantic imagery, Plant initiates his lyric by directly addressing the object of his affections: "Well there's a light in your eye that keeps shining, like a star that can't wait for the night." Then, capitalizing on his starlight reference, he expresses mild concern with a question: "I hate to think I've been blinded baby; why can't I see you tonight?" It's refreshing that we can easily understand Plant's singing voice as he speaks to us with unmistakable enunciation. The reality of the Zeppelin catalog is that this is often not the case. At this point, Plant finishes the first verse with, "And I'm shaking so much with a yearning; why don't you show up and make it all right?" The rhythm section finishes their fourth pass through the main riff before we hear two more played instrumentally and that concludes the basic form of "Fool."

The second verse begins at 1:00 with the same format, but unlike the rather unadorned latter verses in "In the Evening," there is a nice variation heard in the middle of Plant's lyrics. While he intones, "And you thought it was only in movies, as you wish all your dreams would come true," Page inserts an acoustic guitar part that sits nicely atop the main riff. He plays up and down single notes of each chord using what are called arpeggios, giving the music a somewhat Spanish flavor. This is also an excellent example of the polyrhythms present in "Fool" in which the various parts exist in their own time signature but still come into mathematical alignment on important beats.

The third verse, beginning at 1:44, gives us the first glimpse of the street scene as viewed by our protagonist: "Now I will stand in the rain on the corner; I'll watch the people go shuffling downtown." We aren't aware of it yet, but Plant sets us up for a punchline by adding, "Another ten minutes no longer and then I'm turning around." During the next lyrics Page again adds his Spanish arpeggios just as he did previously. At 2:05 Plant drops in an unexpected tie-in to his "eyes that keep shining" opening lyric when he sings, "And the storm that I thought would blow over clouds the light of the love that I found."

At 2:25, Zeppelin embarks on a completely unprecedented maneuver by breaking into a Latin samba rhythm. This is set up by the main riff holding on the fifth scale degree, which creates anticipation for whatever comes next. To supplement the humor of what is about to come, Bonham (most likely) blows hard on a whistle before Jones sets up the new rhythm. Playing unaccompanied piano, Jones pounds on a chord pattern full of syncopation and dynamic interest. The dollop of reverb added to the piano gives the music an outdoor quality as if we are at a fair or sporting event (which explains the whistle). Page and Bonham bound in at 2:35 but it is clearly the percussion that is in charge. The guitar is nearly obliterated by the wall of drums and active piano parts, especially when Plant adds some improvisational phrases that grab our attention. The words he sings are less important than the overall effect of his sustained notes and open vowels. It is fun to imagine how Zeppelin would have approached this animated portion of "Fool" in a concert because it never happened. In 2005, Plant sat in with Pearl Jam for a Katrina fundraiser and they refreshingly chose this song to entertain the $1,000-per-ticket audience. The result was acceptable but would have been difficult for Zeppelin to duplicate with Jones being limited to bass pedals while playing the crucial keyboard parts. They got away with it on "No Quarter," "Stairway to Heaven," and "Kashmir" but those songs did not have bass parts as integral as those found in "Fool."

Zeppelin continues with their samba excursion (even taking advantage of the marimba they found at ABBA's recording studio) until Bonham powers over the wild melee with a vicious drum fill at 3:41 that leads us back to the main riff. When the song began, the main riff came off as rather robust, but returning to it now there is a sense of spacious calm. It must be mentioned that the level of musicianship required of

Jones and Bonham to play what was just heard is not typical of four-piece rock bands. Usually, an army of studio musicians would have been called in to create the aura of what Zeppelin pulled off with primarily just two of their four members. The normally dominant Page was comfortable playing a lesser role knowing the end result was some of their finest playing on record. Of course, this didn't stop Page from contributing a solo with a few shining moments.

As Page's solo begins at 3:52, the most immediate aspect we hear is the unusual timbre of his guitar. Page has always enjoyed finding accessories (the Gizmotron or violin bows) and cutting-edge special effects for his guitar and on "Fool" he uses a device that doubles his guitar one octave lower. The result is that we hear what sounds like two guitars, one playing high and one playing low, shadowing each other. Up to 4:10 we hear Page playing in his tuneful manner that we could easily sing along with after a few listenings. It's when he picks up the pace in this solo that things don't work in his favor. Page is an excellent melody maker and equally as skilled with blues-based, string-bending passion. But finesse at speed is not his forte and when he kicks into a double-time figure at 4:10 his weakness is revealed. The problem is exacerbated by the doubling device that requires extremely accurate playing in order for the melody to be accurately tracked. As soon as Page slips into speed work, his usually charming imperfections become painfully fumbled attempts. At 4:22, he briefly collects himself for a few sanguine moments but can't stop himself from soon churning out the sloppiest solo playing found on any Zeppelin recording. When their entire catalog is weighed as consistently high-grade playing, it's surprising some of these guitar passages were left intact, especially having just heard the musical apex delivered by Jones and Bonham. Oddly enough, the licks Page whips out between 4:35 and 4:45 are some of his coolest on record, but they aren't enough to tip the scales. Taken as a complete solo, Page should have spent more time in the studio improving this one and less time involved with his extracurricular distractions.

As Page's solo wraps up, Plant enters at 4:57 with the final verse. After sharing that he is breathless and palm-sweaty looking for the girl that doesn't come, he hits us with the clincher: "The thoughts of a fool's kind of careless; I'm just a fool waiting on the wrong block." All of his angst about the tardy woman was of his own making. Meanwhile, to make the accompaniment of the last verse unique, Page carries over the guitar track used for his solo by playing aggressive, sustained tones that add weight to the lyrical message. This verse avoids the Spanish-style arpeggios that are delayed as an outro jam beginning at 5:26. Jones's bass line is just as active as Page's acoustic guitar, and together they deliver a breezy variant to the chords used in the main riff. And through it all Bonham steadily beats away with his shuffle pattern, which is impervious to any polyrhythmic intrusions. Plant joins in with a few repetitions of "light of the love that I found" before sustaining the last word on the pitch that is the "home" key center. Normally, this last note isn't notable except that Page and Jones end their last chord based on the fifth note of the major scale, which actually clashes with Plant's note. This is a prime example of giving us what we want (Plant) while leaving us slightly dissatisfied even if we don't know why (Page and Jones).

Unbeknownst to Zeppelin or the world, "Fool" was their last single released while all four members were still alive. The song rose to number 21 on the American charts in February of 1980, proving that a band formed in the twilight of the 1960s could indeed be relevant two decades later. They had survived disco, middle of the road, adult contemporary, punk, and the beginnings of new wave, and still maintained a sound that was immediately recognizable and never too far removed from their earliest work. Good arrangements, excellent musicianship, lyrics that could be serious or tongue in cheek, powerful singing, and melodic guitar solos are attributes heard on the first Zeppelin album right on through to their last and "Fool in the Rain" sustains their legacy.

"Carouselambra"

Lasting over ten and a half minutes, "Carouselambra" is second only to "In the Time of My Dying" as the longest song Zeppelin produced in the studio. It rates as their most progressive of rockers and is a likely indicator of where the band was headed as they approached the 1980s. Constructed primarily by Jones, "Carouselambra" is dominated by synthesizers but contains some indispensable mood-setting from Page, a convincing melody from Plant, and drumming of epic proportions.

The opening notes on synthesizer fall flat and have not stood the test of time. They have a dated quality that is always a risk when incorporating new technology. It may sound fresh for a year or two but then becomes forever associated with a particular timeframe (this was a much more prevalent problem on Plant's first several solo albums in the 1980s). Fortunately, only a few seconds later Jones adds a more dominant keyboard track that is punchy and clean in any decade. And with him is Page laying down timeless, hard-edged guitar chords while Bonham provides drummers everywhere yet another clinic on dropping a solid back-beat pattern right in the rhythmic pocket. In a surprising harmonic shift, the main keyboard riff moves up to an atypical interval as Plant begins to sing. This specific chord movement is referred to by music theorists as "third relations" and was a well-known device for twentieth-century composers to avoid cliché harmonic movement. Jones used the same two chords as the main progression in "Southbound Saurez" so coming up with unusual harmonies was clearly on his mind for the *In Through the Out Door* sessions although he delves deeper on "Carouselambra."

When Plant enters at 0:21 and we listen to the first few lyrics, two things become apparent. First, his voice is mixed low when compared to the keyboards. This was not typical of Zeppelin but was apparently a purposeful choice on "Carouselambra" so that the meaning of his lyrics would be transmitted more on a metaphysical level. Second, because of the complexity of Plant's lyrics and his enunciations, exactly what he is singing is anyone's guess. Official lyrics are not available so you are left to your own conclusions based on listening repeatedly and Internet sources. Making a leap of good faith, let's assume his opening phrase is "Sisters of the wayside bide their time in quiet peace, await their place within the ring of calm," followed by "Still stand to turn in seconds of release, await the call they know may never come." These samples are given to make the point that Plant is completely abandoning the simple directness of "Fool in the Rain" or sketches of painful inner longing found in "All of My Love." On "Carouselambra" Plant is executing his right to be as poetically oblique as he wants. He is not writing lyrics for the general population to comprehend and find enlightenment. These are words between himself and an unnamed party, so find whatever meaning you can, but don't expect overt clarity. Instead, choose to enjoy the overall sensational groove and musicianship as the words wash over you. This is often the best way to listen to rock that leans toward the progressive stylings of Yes, Genesis, Pink Floyd, and Rush.

At 0:30 the chord moves back to the starting position and the tension of the third relation is temporarily resolved but the cycle will be repeated many more times throughout "Carouselambra." Direct your ears to the bass line throughout the verse and you will hear some of Jones's most animated playing. No unflattering bass foot pedals here. Jones weaves through the chords with playful syncopation straight from the James Jamerson playbook. Although his keyboard playing attracts more attention in "Carouselambra," his bass playing reminds us that he is one of the finest practitioners of the instrument.

It is hard to miss the energy in the transition at 1:00. The band hits hard in a manner reminiscent of "Achilles Last Stand" and chokes off the music for a quick pause. Of course this only builds expectation for their return and Zeppelin delivers as advertised with a move to a chord we have yet to hear in "Carouselambra." There is then a return home before one more third relation that starts another verse at 1:19 and the entire progression begins again.

Have you noticed that Page has yet to step out of the shadows? A new riff begins at 2:07 and halfway through the guitar moves ever so closer to the forefront but is quickly pulled back when Plant begins another verse. Page is biding his time and allowing Jones to run the show. The secondary riff returns at 3:13 but his guitar is still held in reserve. In the meantime, there is an intriguing musical discourse that begins at 3:28. First, Jones mimics orchestral strings on his synthesizer playing a friendly melody over new chords. Then, there is a return to the secondary riff and this begins a conversation between the two sections. Each time we hear the strings the melody is developed or altered in some way and because the secondary riff is played several times, we become accustomed to the growing presence of Page's guitar. He is ready to step into the light.

At 4:07 the keyboards finally subside and Page begins playing broken chords (arpeggios) using a bright but clean timbre while Jones plays what is called a "pedal point" on the electric bass. This simply means that while one instrument is moving through a series of chords, the bass remains static on one note (the main riff in "Kashmir" is an excellent example of pedal point). The result is a combination of relaxation (the bass) and movement (the guitar) that provides a welcomed variation in both the harmony and rhythm. Even though this section would be en-

tirely acceptable as the song's "bridge," it turns out Zeppelin is only
using it as a transition to an even more stimulating destination.

In one of the few known instances of Page using the twelve-stringed
half of his double-necked guitar in the recording studio, at 4:25 in
"Carouselambra" Page unleashes brooding power chords as Bonham
slips into a half-time groove. Slow, distorted, and slightly disturbing,
this is grunge before Seattle ever saw it coming. The same two third-
relation chords from the verse are used but here they create a remark-
ably different vibe that is perfect for a night of whiskey, weed, and
questionable decision-making. The band slips back to the pedal-point
section at 5:11 and, with the clean guitar timbre and chords based on a
major scale, it's like the clouds open up to a postcard-perfect day of
sunshine and smiles. But the joy is short lived when the grunge is back
at 5:24. If a battle is being waged between the sinister and the fey, it is
too soon to predict the outcome. Never one to miss out on lyrics about
quests and noble battles, Plant takes full advantage of Page's grim music
when he sings, "Dull is the armor; cold is the day; hard was the journey;
dark was the way." The two sides continue their contest for dominance
when the pedal point and grunge each make another appearance beginning at 6:11. This time Plant strangely shifts to the first person for the
first time in the song and sings, "I heard the word; I couldn't stay; oh I
couldn't stand it another day." He's off for a journey of his own as the
pulsing synthesizer grows up from the grunge at around 7:00 and rams
us headlong into a new section of the song. To introduce new material
this far into a rock composition is risky business but Zeppelin has always
been willing to operate along the border of confident and arrogant.

At this point, and until the song's end, Jones is fully in control. Not
only is he playing the main riff on a synthesizer, but also his electric bass
has been replaced by a funky keyboard. Even some of the lead solo
interjections are played on his Moog synth, leaving Page with less to do
but play background chords. Plant offers a final suggestion to "take of
the fruit, but guard the seed" and the music begins a long fade over the
last thirty seconds of the recording. For those who primarily only like
Zeppelin because of their guitar-hero worship for Jimmy Page, "Carouselambra" is a step in the wrong direction and it raised several concerns
that Jones, with Plant on his side, was staging a coup within the group.
After the band's demise it would be Plant who ultimately held all the
power as to if and when they would perform under the Zeppelin flag.

Page, who is the founding force behind the band's origin and has worked for decades valiantly maintaining the Zeppelin brand, has learned the hard way that Plant has veto power over any new projects. So, for those who saw red flags with the rise of Plant and Jones on songs like "Carouselambra," "Fool in the Rain," and especially "All of My Love," they were likely dead right. Perhaps Page would have pondered the example of guitarist Ritchie Blackmore, who left his band Deep Purple when bassist Glenn Hughes and vocalist David Coverdale started getting a little too funky. To quote a Pink Floyd lyric, "If the band you're in starts playing different tunes, I'll see you on the dark side of the moon."

9

LEFTOVERS

As a performing band, Led Zeppelin closed for business on December 4, 1980. As a money-making machine, the doors were thrown wide open. Owing their record company one more album, the band released *Coda* in 1982 containing a menagerie of outtakes from their twelve years of recording sessions. Two of the eight tracks were actually lifted from a 1970 concert at the Royal Albert Hall with Page re-recording the guitar parts and eliminating the sounds of the audience. These two were joined by a smattering of songs of varied quality with titles such as "Poor Tom" and "Bonzo's Montreaux." The riff-driven "Darlene" and "Wearing and Tearing" offered better representations of Zeppelin's grandeur, but overall this collection of cast-offs strikes many fans as a "coda" that leaves the band's legacy wanting. It is better than nothing, but hardly surmises the depth and quality of their previous albums.

"We're Gonna Groove" was a favorite concert-opening song for Led Zeppelin during their earliest period so it is fitting the song finally finds its way onto an official album. Perhaps only a version of "Train Kept A-Rollin'" would better capture the spirit of those first forays as a new band. Page honors the song by taking the time to improve and build on his original guitar parts and the result is aggressive and gritty, in the best of ways. For a closer look into "We're Gonna Groove," see below.

In the entirety of Zeppelin's back catalog, "Poor Tom" undoubtedly contains the most story-like of Plant's lyrics. We get the complete tale of Tom, including a beginning, middle, and end of the hardworking seventh son. All he wanted was an easy peace after working the railroad, but that evil woman, Annie Mae, made him do wrong. "Tom stood, a gun in his hand, and stopped her runnin' around," sings Plant. The three-minute song hangs mostly on one chord throughout and the drone is animated by Bonham's lively snare-drum shuffle. "Poor Tom" is one more example of how many times Bonzo made a simple song measurably better.

The rendition of "I Can't Quit You Baby" on *Led Zeppelin* is good, very good. But the version on *Coda* is better. The live version from January 9, 1970, jumps out of the speakers with more presence and power. When Zeppelin recorded their first album in October 1968 they had been together barely one month but over the next year "I Can't Quit You Baby" had gestated into a monster of a blues tune with all four members fully contributing. This is the highlight of *Coda*. For a closer look into "I Can't Quit You Baby," see below.

"Walter's Walk" started as a basic track during the *Houses of the Holy* sessions but came to fruition in Page's Sol Studio in 1982. There's just something about the guitar and vocal parts that doesn't match the style and timbre used by both musicians in 1972. Page's guitar is much more similar to his work in the post-Zeppelin era than to "Celebration Day" or "The Crunge." And the excessive reverb on Plant's voice was never used on any other Zeppelin recording, so why would it suddenly show up on "Walter's Walk" if not to mask the fact that he is singing with a voice ten years gone from the original session? The melody is too static to attract great attention and is anchored primarily on Plant whining about "walking the floor" over a woman. The guitar solo is equally lacking in originality. It's Jones and Bonham to the rescue as they lock in together as a fierce rhythm section.

"Ozone Baby" resulted from the *In Through the Out Door* sessions of 1978 but, after hearing the song, you'll see that the style didn't match anything else on the album and why it made sense to save the track for later. As we have heard on several Zeppelin tracks over the years that have a defined vocal chorus, Plant leans heavily on the handy convenience of needing, wanting, sharing, or finding love. "Out on the Tiles," "All of My Love," "Whole Lotta Love," "In the Evening," "Wearing and Tearing," and now "Ozone Baby" all make the list. In any one of those songs the subject matter is adequate but since *Coda* was meant to be the final album, it's a shame Plant didn't mix it up more often while he had the chance.

"Darlene" is five minutes of a whole lot of fun. Plant had never featured one woman's name so prominently in a lyric and doesn't hold anything back pleading his way through each chorus. The punchy riff and sassy piano are enough to make this song jump, but the swinging second half kicks "Darlene" into the upper echelon of Zeppelin rockers. In many ways, this throwback was ahead of its time. For a closer look at "Darlene," see below.

If you've ever had the pleasure of seeing Rush in concert, you likely witnessed the incredible drummer Neil Peart perform a drum solo featuring a mountain of acoustic and electric drums allowing him to create not only rhythms but also sweeping melodies and entire orchestrations. None of this equipment existed in Bonham's day but he made use of what was available in the far-reaching "Bonzo's Montreaux." Beginning with conventional drum patterns played in the indelible Bonham fashion, the unaccompanied drummer shifts into playing electronic pitches triggered by his drums. In this way, Bonham is able to play recognizable melodies suitable for humming while hammering away at the foot-heavy drum beats he loved. Recorded in 1976, the piece didn't find a home on *Presence* or *In Through the Out Door* but on *Coda* was a suitable tribute to a man who is often called the greatest of all rock drummers.

"Wearing and Tearing" has the auspicious title as the "broom wagon" song in the recorded career of Led Zeppelin. The parade is over and now begins the sweeping up. Don't look for a hidden gem or secret backward-masked farewell message. But you will hear Zeppelin's response to being called "dinosaurs" by the punks in the late 1970s. "Wearing and Tearing" sounds as fast as anything they ever recorded and only the verses allow a respite. It's hard to know for sure what Plant is singing but he poignantly asks, "What's that creeping up behind you? It's just an old friend, and what's that he's got for you?" Perhaps the answer is fellowship, or drugs, or music, or light and shade. Legend claims that "Wearing and Tearing" was going to be released as a single in time for the 1979 concerts at Knebworth. The Zeppelin fans of the day would have dug it. But the punks would have ripped it to shreds as a bunch of old tarts messing with something they don't understand. "Wearing and Tearing" is far from Zeppelin's best work, but it's still too good to have been compared to punk and it's just as well the release was delayed until a later day when the arguments no longer mattered.

A CLOSER LOOK

"We're Gonna Groove"

The liner notes on *Coda* cite "We're Gonna Groove" as being recorded at Morgan Studios in London during the month of June 1969 but it isn't true. The drums, bass, and vocals were taken from a live recording made during a concert at the Royal Albert Hall on January 9, 1970. Careful listening to that performance on the *Led Zeppelin* DVD reveals how Plant, Jones, and Bonham play exactly the same as is heard on the *Coda* version. Given the improvisational nature of these musicians, it is not conceivable that they would duplicate every nuance of an unreleased studio version one year later at a concert. For unknown reasons, Zeppelin wanted to disguise the origins of "We're Gonna Groove" when *Coda* was released in 1982. Perhaps there were questions about the recording rights or they didn't want to admit at the time that the Albert Hall concert had been recorded. Or, more likely, Page wasn't willing to leave the original guitar parts alone and the new overdubs wouldn't jibe with a recording known to be from a live concert. Regardless, the track was dusted off by Page in 1982 when looking for *Coda* material and "We're Gonna Groove" was selected for good reason. The song had already been road tested as the opener during concerts across Europe and America the first half of 1970 and bootlegs were very popular. "We're Gonna Groove" had become the mythical white whale to Zeppelin fans. Everyone seemed to know someone who had a friend with a copy, but it never officially materialized until Page decided to work some post-production magic and reveal it to the world once and for all.

Page's efforts would include completely scrapping the original guitar part, recording several guitar overdubs, editing out a jam session, and skillfully mixing the recording to sound like a studio track rather than a concert performance. To achieve the latter, the audio of the retained instruments and vocals was taken directly from the mixing board as opposed to microphones placed at a distance from the musicians meant to pick up the ambiance of the room and audience. The unfortunate sacrifice is that Bonham's drums sound much better on the concert DVD than on *Coda*. The fullness of his drum kit as it reverberates throughout the Royal Albert Hall is chopped off at the knees for the faux-studio version. Plant and Jones fare much better and Page's revised guitars are far superior to what he played in concert some twelve years earlier.

Imagine yourself at the Royal Albert Hall on January 9, 1970, about to hear your favorite rock band begin their set. You have been looking forward to the concert for weeks and cued up at the ticket window hours before it opened in order to gain access before the show sells out. Then, on the night of the event, you make sure to wear your coolest clothes including a Zeppelin t-shirt from a previous tour. You bring along a new copy of *Led Zeppelin II* just in case you are able to slip back stage after the final encore and convince a roadie to let you seek an autograph from one or two of the band members. Of course, getting backstage is an easier proposition if you happen to be an attractive young lady. If not, maybe a little cash or grass will do the trick. As the lights dim on the stage you can make out a few long-haired figures making their way to their instruments. The audience becomes electric with anticipation as someone, it must be Bonham, whips off a quick drum fill and does some last-minute adjusting. The lights come up and there is the golden-haired vocalist with his slightly mischievous grin, half-smoked cigarette in hand, calmly addressing you with a characteristic "Good evenin'," and the audience erupts in response. Bang! Bonham hits his snare eight times in a precise rhythm as Page and then Jones jump in just behind. The rocking has begun and you look at your friends around you (even if you just met them) reveling in the common experience everyone in the room is sharing. The drum beat is frantic with Keith Moon–like fills, Jones is laying down a wickedly complex but perfectly played bass line, Plant is thrusting his exposed chest while gripping the microphone in preparation for his first verse, and Page prowls his corner of the stage looking every inch the swaggering guitar hero (on his twenty-sixth birthday no less).

Page opens up "We're Gonna Groove" with what many guitarists know as the "Purple Haze" chord. The formal designation is a dominant seventh chord with an added sharp ninth and Jimi Hendrix made such effective use of it on "Purple Haze" and "Foxy Lady" that it became associated with him as a trademark. But it is such a great rock-and-roll chord that other guitarists must be forgiven for the occasional trespass and that includes Page at the Royal Albert Hall.

Plant brings the microphone to his lips and angrily sings, "Hear my baby comin' down the track; betcha my baby's comin' back." This is followed immediately by the optimistic but equally aggressive "Someday she'll get back to me; we're gonna raise a family." This lyric was taken from the song "Groovin'" by Ben E. King (co-written by James Bethea), whose live version for Atlantic Records surpasses Zeppelin's attempt simply because the brass section played like soul-soaked lunatics. Although, while King is content to sing about his lady in a desirously heartfelt manner, Plant tears into Zeppelin's rendition with his nether regions in flames. He doesn't just *hope* his love interest is coming back; he *expects* it and will be exacting a costly toll for any other outcome. Plant delivers us to the first chorus after only twenty-eight seconds when he sings, "We're gonna groove, yeah groove," and concludes with the hook, "we're gonna love, love, love, 'til the break of day" (King ends his chorus with *dawn*). Many girls in the Albert Hall crowd no doubt imagine themselves as the object of his exultations, but whoever the conquest of Plant's desires may be, she is in for a long night. Or, taken metaphorically, Plant is announcing in the opening song of the concert that the band is fired up and ready to jam with the audience until the sun rises or the coppers come.

When listening to the *Coda* version rather than the concert, the ominously low guitar tones heard during the chorus were just one of the several tracks Page added in 1982. He is using the same octave-doubling device as is heard on the solo to "Fool in the Rain." In that solo, the low octave was problematic as Page unsuccessfully attempted to finesse his way through the fast passages, but on "We're Gonna Groove" he limits himself to banging out sustained power chords and the effect is palpable. Page creates an added sense of lurking menace that greatly supports the angst of Plant's vocal attitude.

At the 1970 Albert Hall performance, Zeppelin finished the second chorus of "We're Gonna Groove" and did indeed find their groove by Page playing a solo over the form of the verse and chorus before directing the band into a breakdown jam. Plant then wails a few improvisational phrases and wordless swoops as the energy picks up over the "Purple Haze" chord. The band proceeds to bounce off the eight-hit pattern as heard during the introduction and then it's onward to the final verse and chorus. What Page does for the *Coda* rendition of "We're Gonna Groove" in order to mask the telltale signs of a live concert is quite clever. He completely removes the chorus portion of the solo and vocal-oriented breakdown that follows. Instead, he splices eight measures of the solo verse with the last eight measures of the jam that occurs after the vocal breakdown (all with the original guitar removed). In this way, we hear a solo that begins at 1:16 and lasts for a total of sixteen measures before the rehashing of the introduction material. Because the chorus section is removed, the harmony never moves from the key center used for the verse and this allows Page to orchestrate a multi-layered solo that dives and bends without ever having to adjust to changing chords. Since the total runtime of *Coda*'s "We're Gonna Groove" is only 2:39, editing the solo to allow Page to develop a mood uninterrupted by the chorus section was, while not true to the live performance, artistically satisfying in the context of a version meant to mimic an in-studio recording. And Page goes to great lengths to turn this wild-charging concert opener into a semi-controlled composition by recording at least four guitar tracks in the solo section. On two of them Page plays lead, on one he lays down chord rhythms, and on the fourth he drops the occasional octave-divided bomb. Accumulatively, this exemplifies the mastery that occurs when Page takes the time in the studio to process his creativity.

At 1:52, Plant is back to tell us (redundantly) how his girl is "Sweet as sweet as sweet can be." He then closes out the verse with words that are made completely believable by his sultry, pent-up delivery: "You just set my soul on fire; woman you know you're my one desire." The band begins the first of two choruses at 2:08 that drive home their unflinching mission to groove right up until the final moment. Even their final chord plays with us in two ways. First, Page employs a last attempt to convince us this is a studio recording by adding a low synthesizer note that fades out with the guitars. Second, the last chord is not the "home" harmony so we are left with a sense of incompletion that makes us want to hear more. Always more.

"I Can't Quit You Baby"

"I Can't Quit You Baby" is the second track from *Coda* in which Zeppelin attempted to disguise the origins, although in this case they stayed closer to the truth than with "We're Gonna Groove." For "I Can't Quit You Baby," the album notes document the song as being recorded live on January 9, 1970, Royal Albert Hall (all true) but during a daytime sound check instead of the evening concert (not true). Zeppelin was peculiarly concerned with hiding the fact that the concert had been recorded, even though their later releases proved the undoing of this self-created myth.

Compared to the severe edits and overdubs Page slashed into "We're Gonna Groove," he was quite gentle with the editorial treatment of "I Can't Quit You Baby" and this is likely due to not trying to hide the fact that the recording was made in a one-take, live situation. Rather than add more in the way of layered guitar tracks, he primarily just trimmed off the edges of the recording in order to condense the runtime and remove audience applause.

On *Coda*, "I Can't Quit You Baby" begins without the lengthy introduction heard at the Royal Albert Hall performance and elsewhere. During concerts, Zeppelin had come up with a unique introduction to "I Can't Quit You Baby" in which they begin playing a slow blues three pitches lower. After Page solos for ten measures, the band stops the rhythm and slides up three chords until arriving at the key of "I Can't Quit You Baby" and then they let the notes fade out until Plant brings them back in. The vocalist improvises a few phrases and then, tuning in on the pitch of the last chord played, Plant sings the song title in a patient and mournful tone as the band comes thundering in behind him. It makes for a ripping good introduction. But, at the whim of Page's production choices, the opening material is dropped in favor of jumping right to Plant's lead-in phrase similar to the way it is heard on their first album. And until the concert DVD was released over twenty years later, no one but the most ardent of bootleg owners was the wiser.

The strength of "I Can't Quit You Baby" as heard on the *Led Zeppelin* album is that it features the band playing live with no overdubs. It demonstrated from the very first record that this was a quartet of musicians who could play their own instruments without the aid of any outside hired guns. The members of Zeppelin *were* the hired guns. And after playing the song consistently for two years, they only became more confident in their skills. For this reason, the *Coda* version is much stronger than the debut studio recording. Bonham is the most obviously improved between the two renditions. If you only listen to the 1968 take, he sounds like a drummer in full command and willing to take chances. But after hearing the 1970 rendition on *Coda*, you realize how much more aggressive he became. In comparison, his earlier attempt comes off as downright timid. Plant too shows more growth and comfort delivering the Willie Dixon blues lyric. He sells it hard, at one point (1:20) literally shaking his entire body into the microphone during the phrase "You build my hopes so high; then you let me down." And Jones on the bass is simply rock solid. In fact, when Page goes astray it is Jones that lays down the law and pulls the guitarist into alignment. This musical brotherhood did not yet exist during their 1968 recording session but was well developed only two years later after several tours of the United Kingdom, Europe, and the United States.

As for Mr. Page, he delivers a stunner of a solo, all the more impressive when it was made obvious in the later DVD that he played it all live with no inserted corrections. In fact, a glaring mistake was made, and Page had the maturity in 1982 to leave the track alone, knowing that it wouldn't diminish the accumulative dignity of his lead playing. Listen at 2:51 as the band is supposed to hit the "home" chord and then slide up one step to another chord that creates a sense of tension. This harmonic movement is played at the end of each twelve-measure form and begins on the less-expected second beat of the measure. This presents difficulty when Page is playing with no overdubbed guitars because he must remember to break off from his solo with enough time to become his own rhythm guitarist and hit those two power chords. Then he solos some more before hitting the two chords once again at 2:56. On the *Led Zeppelin* album he navigates through the corresponding obstacle course effectively. On the first version of "I Can't Quit You Baby" from the *BBC Sessions* he blows the first two hits by coming in late before recovering for the next set (2:04). On the second *BBC Sessions* take of the same song Page is fine. But for the *Coda* rendition he trips up twice. At 2:51 he plays the power chord on the correct beat but his hand is on the wrong fret, forcing him to noticeably move upward in pitch. Thrown off by his mistake, Page aggressively attacks the next two-chord set at 2:56 only to come in too early. Meanwhile, Jones and Bonham don't flinch at all and Page settles in as the three of them move collectively ahead.

Page should be acknowledged for having the guts to leave his musical indiscretion on *Coda* for all to hear, especially because it is surrounded by some of his finest blues soloing on record. The full range of his humanity is expressed in a solo that achieves supreme heights while visiting a brief low. Conversely, Page should also be admonished for giving in to his ego when the DVD version of this track was released decades later. Find your way to the corresponding moment of the video performance and you will hear that the two missteps have magically repaired themselves. It is no mistake that the camera angle chosen for that exact moment is from Page's back so that we can't see his hand on the wrong chord or the right chord at the wrong time. Hats off to Page in 1982 for making the right call. Too bad he didn't leave his artistically acceptable imperfections alone in 2003.

"Darlene"

As the 1970s gave way to the next decade, rock music was looking for inspiration. Disco had run its course as a dance and fashion statement. Punk music had made a mark but would only cross over to the mainstream in diluted form. New Wave and synth pop were still a few years ahead when keyboard technology became cheap enough for the masses. And the biggest rock bands had been saddled with the offensive "dinosaur" label. So, a handful of musicians did what their creed has always done to move ahead: look to the past. In this case, swinging rockabilly was the medicine to cure the blues at the cusp of 1980.

Queen was the first band to score big on the charts with a retro-rocker. Their release of "Crazy Little Thing Called Love" in late 1979 resulted in a number 1 hit in America and vast worldwide sales. Freddie Mercury wrote the song but, with his limited guitar skills, the chords were quite simple (considering this is the band who gave us "Bohemian Rhapsody"). The stripped-down and swinging feel is what gives "Crazy Little Thing" its timeless appeal. Queen songs like "Radio Ga Ga" or "Another One Bites the Dust" have production values that are forever associated with the years they came out. But "Crazy Little Thing" could have been written and recorded in any decade, thereby making it evergreen. With the exception of the top-notch solo of Brian May, this is a tune any modestly skilled guitarist can strum and sing around a campfire. In the wake of 1970s "art rock" that only virtuosos dared play, or disco music never meant to be performed outside of a studio, the sweet simplicity of "Crazy Little Thing" resonated with an audience who wanted their music to feel more inclusive.

Following the lead of Queen, a "new" band emerged on the scene in 1982 with a smash hit, "Rock This Town." The Stray Cats placed the song in the top ten on the American charts and the singer/guitarist has forged a decades-long career out of the image of a pompadour hipster with a swinging six-string. Whether in a trio or big band, Brian Setzer proved the long-term marketability of a simple, guitar-driven rhythm supported by a back-beat shuffle and walking bass line.

It turns out Zeppelin was ahead of the curve, even if no one (including the band) knew it at the time. Beating "Rock this Town" by eighteen months and "Crazy Little Thing Called Love" by six, Led Zeppelin recorded their own swinging rocker called "Darlene." It's not as catchy as the hook Queen came up with, and it doesn't have one user-friendly riff like "Rock This Town," but it does have serious groove and an obvious sense of playfulness. A teenaged guitarist can listen to "Darlene" and rightly say, "That sounds cool and I bet I could play that."

"Darlene" was written and recorded during the *In Through the Out Door* sessions in November 1978. Deciding it wouldn't improve the album, it was set aside for inclusion on a future project. It's true that "Darlene" does not rate over tracks like "In the Evening" or "Carouselambra," but to be displaced by a poorly played and ill-conceived train wreck like "Hot Dog" makes no sense. There may also have been a problem related to minutes on the clock. "Hot Dog" is almost two minutes shorter than "Darlene" and there just wasn't any room left on side 1 of *In Through the Out Door*. Another explanation for the exclusion of "Darlene" is the lyric. The words Plant sings smack of being a first-draft effort as if he were singing nothing but placeholder lyrics and there just wasn't time to improve the product like he would normally do. Considering the depth and cohesion of the lyrics that made the cut for the album, "Darlene" was a step below. Words like "I don't care what people say and I don't care what they do; sweet child I gotta make you mine; you're the only thing that I want: you" are hardly fresh, let alone grammatically sound. So while "Darlene" didn't meet the band's subjective qualifications for *In Through the Out Door*, it was good enough for the leftovers of *Coda*.

The first eight seconds of "Darlene" are classic Zeppelin. The rhythm section enters together pounding out three heavy chords moving upward with some dexterous riffing in between. There are a few journalists who question the production quality of the music derived from the Polar recording studio but there is no obvious shortcoming on "Darlene." The drums are fat and both Page and Jones sound forceful. The piano sounds slightly out of tune but the honky-tonk charm it adds isn't out of place. The introduction is also effective in that it sounds like

Zeppelin is supposed to sound, but we aren't given enough information to really know what kind of rhythmic feel the song is about. We have been handed a present but can't see through the wrapping.

When the main riff begins at 0:09, it is not a letdown. While Page and Jones play three spacious hits moving downward (providing a nice contrast to the introduction) followed by a more active turnaround riff, Bonham plays in a relaxed half-time feel and the combination of the two components combine for a funky, dare-we-call-it-hip-hop groove. Under it all Jones plays a piano that bashes out the rhythmic subdivision and gives the track a classic R&B flavor. After a break in the music, Plant introduces us to the namesake of the song at 0:19 by keeping it simple with, "Darlene, ooh Darlene, ooh Darlene, ooh yeah" spread over four measures. For lack of a better term, this functions as the chorus and it's a creative switch to place it first and the verse second. Beginning at 0:44, the first verse moves to a new chord that is slid into from below with a repeating syncopation that leaves space around it for Plant's vocals and some bluesy piano fills. At 0:56 the cycle begins anew and we hear another chorus and verse with only a touch more guitar to set it apart.

After the second verse, Page breaks into a solo at 1:32 over the chords used for the chorus and it's good, rollicking fun. Even though "Darlene" is a throwback to an older style, Page is using the string-bending and sustained notes that epitomize his later Zeppelin days. Plant would have benefited from revisiting his vocal parts at a later date but Page captures a fully developed solo with all the elements that Page fans want to hear. His sense of rhythm is accurate, he understands the genre, the timbre of his guitar and amp is excellent, and (unlike many younger improvisers) he knows how to build an arch of interest throughout a solo with a keen sense of knowing how to successfully end his final phrase.

Page cleanly hands off the solo duties at 1:57 to Jones, who surprises us with something he only plays on one other song in the entire Zeppelin studio catalog: an all-out piano solo (the other instance being "No Quarter"). The chords for his accompaniment are taken from the verse but the band is generous to double the normal length so Jones has ample time to strut. Listen for the slick way he concludes his solo at 2:17 with the ascending line played in octaves just like Jerry Lee Lewis. Jones tops it off with a dash of glissando as the band returns to the chords used at the very opening of the song. This time, however, they run through the sequence two times in order to build up a little more tension for what's coming. Take notice of the drum fill Bonham plays at 2:23 and how it differs from the one at 2:31. The first fill is heavy and evenly spaced. The second, however, is full of energy and asks you to pay attention to what's coming. In the tradition of the great big-band drummers like Gene Krupa and Buddy Rich, Bonham is a master of setting up transitions and this is no exception.

Coming into 2:32 is when "Darlene" really takes off. The band kicks up their heels with a full swing tempo of about 160 beats per minute, which is perfect for jitterbug dancing. Plant is in excellent vocal form using a raspy tone reminiscent of his *Presence* recordings and Bonham seems to be having piles of fun playing a classic shuffle back-beat. Jones can be heard occasionally tossing in overdubbed honky-tonk piano fills on top of his bass.

For most of "Darlene" Jones doubles the guitar riff an octave lower but at 3:09 he takes off on his own "walking bass" adventure. This is as close to straight-up big-band music as Zeppelin ever recorded in studio and it is a fine moment. The words Plant is singing are trite or even indistinguishable but the passion of his delivery makes it more than worth hearing. Page does an excellent job "comping" (jazz slang for providing accompaniment) the chords and collectively the band is totally swinging. The only thing missing is the brass and saxophone sections roaring away. It's easy to see the connection between this track and what Plant recorded in 1984 with the Honeydrippers. On their one and only album, "Rockin' at Midnight" was arranged for big band and basically fulfilled the promise made five years earlier by Zeppelin's "Darlene." It's notable that Plant included Brian Setzer in the Honeydrippers project: a guitarist/vocalist that was part of the rockabilly revival Zeppelin helped kindle with their live performances and songs like "Darlene."

From 3:55 through the end of the track, the boys are rocking like young lions again and it is stunning to think that the same blokes swinging their way through these boogie-woogie chords are also responsible for "Rain Song," "Kashmir," "No Quarter," "In the Light," "Carouselambra," "In the Evening," and the giant among giants: "Stairway to Heaven." The diversity within Bonham, Jones, Page, and Plant was exceptional and seldom seen in any rock band of any era. Of course we'll never know what Zeppelin would have done had Bonham not fallen asleep on his back that fateful night, but given the incredible diversity they exhibited right up to the end, anything was possible. Even though they ultimately didn't need "Darlene" for *In Through the Out Door*, it's good to know that even after eleven years of putting up with each other like brothers, roommates, and spouses all rolled into one, they were still able to throw down, rock out, and swing madly.

10

NEW KEYS FOR OLD SINGERS

The members of Led Zeppelin, chiefly Jimmy Page, often described their live performances as wildly improvisational and, when compared to their studio recordings, the better representation of their true power as a rock band. And yet, for decades the only recorded document of their live exploits was the oft-criticized soundtrack to the film *The Song Remains the Same*. If this were to be the only example of Zeppelin onstage, it would have been sadly lacking. Only decades after the group's disbandment did official performance recordings and video become available. 1997 marked the release of the *BBC Sessions*. The multi-CD package documents the earliest days of the band, including an untested ballad about a certain stairway to heaven, but only features performances through April 1971.

Some of their later catalog was heard as live renditions in 2003 with the release of *How the West Was Won*. This three-CD set was recorded in June 1972 and included material from their first five albums. Although this release features far superior performances than *The Song Remains the Same*, Zeppelin fans still had no official releases of material from the band's last three studio albums. Bootlegs of various later concerts began to circulate, especially after public sharing on the Internet became easy and popular, but the sound quality was always inferior to the exacting standards we are used to hearing from official recordings produced by Jimmy Page.

The dearth of a definitive and comprehensive live recording was finally solved thirty-three years after Zeppelin's breakup of the original band. An unprecedented two-hour reunion concert on December 10, 2007, (with John Bonham's son Jason on drums) was presented as a tribute to Ahmet Ertegun, the founder of Atlantic Records, who died at the end of 2006. Video and audio of the concert was eventually released as *Celebration Day* in 2013. The band's legions of fans, including generations too young to have ever experienced the group when they were active, were finally given a contemporary reference point for what Zeppelin was all about.

As much can be gleaned from what they performed as what they chose to omit. The full concert featured sixteen songs and bootleg video confirms that no titles were held back from the official release. Only one song ("Since I've Been Loving You") came from *Led Zeppelin III.* Two songs each were heard from the albums *Led Zeppelin, Led Zeppelin II, Houses of the Holy,* and *Presence. Physical Graffiti,* originally a double album, was well represented by three songs. But *Led Zeppelin IV* was given the most emphasis with four entries. Of course, "Stairway to Heaven," "Rock and Roll," and "Black Dog" were a given (despite Plant's reticence to keep singing the ballad he no longer considers relevant), but "Misty Mountain Hop" was a surprise. And if you haven't noticed yet, nothing from *In Through the Out Door* was performed. Not the epic "In the Evening," not the intense "Carouselambra" (it would have been fun to see Jones working the keyboard and bass parts at the same time), and not even the formulaic radio-friendly hit "All of My Love." Zeppelin was tasked with selecting material across their entire catalog to represent their legacy, and nothing from *In Through the Out Door* was deemed worthy. Considering their swan song album featured the dominance of Jones as a keyboardist and songwriter, he would have every right to feel snubbed, just as he did when Plant and Page joined for an album and tour in the mid-1990s but never bothered to give their old band member a call.

Another extremely telling detail from their reunion concert is the need of Plant, age 59 at the time, to lower the keys to the majority of the songs performed, some originally recorded nearly forty years earlier when he was young and bulletproof. Of the sixteen songs, ten were lowered a full step to accommodate the gracefully aging Plant and he shouldn't be blamed. As a brash twenty-something he set the bar impossibly high. Time and again we hear other artists cover Zeppelin material and cringe at the failure of the vocalists who can't quite match the power and range of Plant. And now, ironically, Plant is facing the same issue of being asked to sing like himself, only without the benefits of youth. There is an old rock-and-roll joke told from the point of view of a groupie who always fantasizes about what a fabulous lover Plant must be even though she had never been with him. No matter what rock star she has relations with, her assessment is always, "He is no Robert Plant." Finally, her dream is fulfilled and she manages to sleep with Plant after a concert, after which she tells her friends the next day, "Well, he was okay, but he's no Robert Plant." It's not easy living up to the reputation of a living legend and just because he could sing those stratospheric notes in the shine of his youth, there are a contingent of fans that will forever hold him accountable to keep doing the same. It's tough being a golden god.

Regardless of the shifting of some keys, the music of *Celebration Day* is exceptional and in follow-up interviews all the players seemed pleased. As the three Zeppelin survivors continue to age and, in the case of Plant, are forced to accommodate new limitations, a reunion tour or album seems increasingly unlikely. As a result, the 2007 concert may ultimately serve as the final documentation of Zeppelin in a full-production performance setting. The songs performed don't represent their entire output, but they do speak to how they might have progressed had they stayed together. Their confidence and command of the music is fully evident. The band's music was under constant development throughout the 1970s and when finally revisited in 2007, Zeppelin reveals several ways they chose to adapt to the times. Upon close examination, the songs of the mighty Zeppelin did not remain the same, but December 10, 2007, was indeed a day worth celebrating.

A CLOSER LOOK

"Good Times, Bad Times"

Somehow, of the estimated 20 million requests, you are one of the eight thousand people chosen from a lottery to purchase one of the sixteen thousand tickets available to the public for the one-off Led Zeppelin concert scheduled for November 26, 2007, at the O2 Arena in London. You were too young to have seen them in the 1970s and the videos you saw of their abbreviated interim performances in 1985, 1988, and 1995 were under-rehearsed and underwhelming. This is the opportunity of a lifetime to see one of the greatest rock bands in history play a complete set with not only the three surviving members but also the son of the departed John Bonham sitting behind the drums. Vacations are requested, hotels are booked, cars are rented, and you are ready to go. Then the troublesome news: "Page Fractures Finger." Fortunately, the concert is not canceled but only postponed two weeks until December 10. After copious rescheduling and rebooking, your attendance at the new date is on track. But this raises one valid question: will Page play well enough or will he allow his nerves to get the best of him (as he is known to do) and blame an injury for the poor outcome? The whole world will be watching this concert and Page, Plant, Jones, and Jason Bonham know the ramifications if they deliver anything less than a stellar performance. In real time as they play, any musical missteps will go viral on the Internet with comments about how they embarrassed themselves as irrelevant dotards. Had they been performing a special-occasion concert or an awards show every few years, the pressure would be diluted, but after their long self-banishment this was the equivalent of an all-in bet. Before the concert is even concluded, they will either thrive as elder statesmen of rock still worthy of their thrones in the pantheon (with the likes of U2, the Eagles, the Rolling Stones, and the Who), or they will be demoted to the heap of once-great bands now relegated to casinos and county fairs (like Journey, Heart, Def Leppard, and REO Speedwagon).

But first, there are the several opening acts that on any other concert ticket would be worthy headliners. On this night however, there is an understood anxiousness to get them up and right back off as soon as possible. The first band is a super-group in their own right including keyboardist legend Keith Emerson, resident Yes-men Chris Squire and Alan White, and Bad Company's Simon Kirke, along with a full brass section. As is the case with opening acts, they look rather disrespected being restricted to the front of the stage and performing in front of a black curtain temporarily hiding the headliner's domain. Strangely enough, this prog-rock menagerie chooses to play a version of "Kashmir" thinking it might tide the audience until the real thing comes along. You and your twenty thousand new friends show an initial spike of interest but it quickly wanes when it is clear no one from Zeppelin is making an early guest appearance.

Next up for the difficult task of placating an audience only there to see Zeppelin (or to be seen, as is the case with many of the celebrities trickling in), is Bill Wyman's Rhythm Kings. Wyman keeps things interesting by featuring several guest artists including Paul Rogers (also from Bad Company, as well as his two-album band with Page, the Firm), Mick Jones from Foreigner, guitarist Alvin Lee from Ten Years After, and vocalist Maggie Bell, who was one of the first signings to Zeppelin's Swan Song record label.

Finally, the overtures are concluded and the main act is soon to take the stage. There are rumblings and gawking as famous guests are directed to their reserved seating including Mick Jagger, Dave Grohl, Marilyn Manson, Kate Moss, Naomi Campbell, Jeff Beck, Paul McCartney, Brian May, Ann Wilson, Dave Mustaine, Peter Gabriel, and the Edge. Well behind this VIP section, from your seat in the middle of the hall you can make out shadowy movements onstage. The audience grows quieter but the tension is coiled like a spring ready to break from its confines. You hear four clicks of drumsticks and with a burst of light the music of Led Zeppelin begins.

Bum-Bump! The first two hits of a low power-chord are all the audience needs to know that the opening song is "Good Times, Bad Times," which, suitably, is Zeppelin's first song on their first album. The concert is beginning the same place their recorded career began thirty-nine years earlier. The lights flash up and down with each successive blast of the two-chord hits until the classic guitar riff and vocals begin at 0:17. The giant video screen behind the stage displays close-ups from many angles and you notice immediately that the boys are looking fit as they move about in tight formation. Unlike many rock bands that spread out to all corners of a stage, Zeppelin is known for close-quarter performance where they can easily hear and communicate with each other.

Also differing from many classic bands that roll out various reunion concerts and tours, you appreciate that Zeppelin has chosen not to use backup musicians. There is no hired-gun phalanx comprised of a rhythm electric guitarist, rhythm acoustic guitarist, acoustic pianist, synthesizer keyboardist, organist, percussionist, and bevy of background vocalists. At their heart, Zeppelin always was and still is a simple rock

trio with a singer and they will either succeed or fail on their own, with
no fluffed up concert ensemble to hide behind.

And even with the advent of in-ear monitoring systems, Zeppelin is
going old school with large speakers across the front of the stage that
allow the band to hear their own mix, which is different from what the
audience hears. In-ear monitors are much preferred because they re-
duce or eliminate piercing feedback problems on stage and you can't
help but notice that is just what's happening. The feedback will clear up
soon enough and you are so excited the show has begun that you are
willing to overlook it. Years later the band would reveal at a press
conference that the monitors were not working properly for the first
few songs but they never let it show at the time.

The main riff on "Good Times" is a wonderful fusion of simple and
complex. The first measure starts with nothing but two swift cannon
strikes followed by three beats of animated drumming. The second
measure is a busy mix up of a chord arpeggio and a syncopated series of
notes that rise back to the beginning of the riff. If you've been paying
attention through the earlier chapters of this book you will have picked
up on the sure bet that busy riffs (think "Black Dog," "The Ocean," and
"In the Evening") are written by Jones. Even though the song is based
firmly on the verse-chorus format Zeppelin shied away from, the riff is
so catchy in its "simple complexity" that it was an instant hit at the end
of 1968 and still rocks you and the entire O2 Arena in 2007.

You are not a trained musician but you dabble at guitar and know
how to play a few Zeppelin riffs so you are greatly enjoying the close-up
of Page as he plays the iconic "Good Times." You can clearly see that his
hands are on the frets you would expect but even in the excitement of
the music you sense something is different between what you are hearing from the stage and what you've heard hundreds of times on your car
stereo. Additionally, as Plant sings the opening phrases you are impressed that he seems to be handling the high notes with a sense of ease
that belies his age, especially when you've heard quality singers much
younger crash and burn on the same song. If the person standing next
to you had perfect pitch she would be able to explain the answer to both
of your perceived curiosities. Zeppelin is playing the song one step
lower than the original recording. This allows Plant to conserve his
voice and shield him from missing the highest notes if he is in any way
not in excellent form. On any one song Plant can probably still warm up

and hit the money notes the same as he ever did, but with sixteen songs back to back, he is professional enough to know that insurances needed to be made. But as a guitarist, you know Page and Jones have their hands on the usual frets so how is it they are playing a lower key than usual? The strings of their instruments are tuned lower, allowing them to play in a Plant-friendly key while still using the fret-board positioning they are most comfortable with. It's a necessary concession for the musicians but the songs end up sounding slightly odd: like tasting a delicious meal but you can't help feeling there's something missing from the recipe that might make it even better. But it's Zeppelin, it's loud in the best of ways, and you're at the most-talked-about concert in years so you shake off the sense of oddness and rock out to more "Good Times, Bad Times."

The great thing about "Good Times" is that even with its brief run-time of around three minutes, the drums, bass, guitar, and vocals all have featured moments so it serves as a convenient way to introduce each band member to the audience. There are several prominent drum fills that John Bonham impressed his peers with all those years before and now you smile with a sense of "chip off the old block" pride when you hear Jason nail them one after another. You are further impressed by Jason when you realize that not only is he tackling the job of one of rock's greatest drummers, but he's also doing it while singing a harmony vocal part (first heard at 0:40). Next to be introduced is Jones on bass at 0:57 when he plays a short solo riff just like you've heard so many times before. You and the audience respond by showing him the appreciation he seldom receives being the "quiet" one in the band. After the first minute you're getting over your initial burst of adrenaline caused by the spectacle of it all and starting to pay closer attention to the music. Plant sings the bridge portion of the song with "At sixteen I fell in love with a girl as sweet as can be" and the shifted key allows him to use the lower register of his voice in a strong and comfortable tone. This is not a local tribute band or even a cover by a known band looking for a marketing gimmick; this is Led Zeppelin in the flesh, and Plant is standing tall and sounding good.

And the last to be introduced to you and the audience that night was the cause of it all. It was Jimmy Page that originally formulated the band in 1968 and here he is in 2007 looking completely natural in his most productive domain. He made a splash with the Firm, recorded an excellent album with David Coverdale, stayed in the news with the Black Crows, and even represented his nation proudly when performing at the Olympic closing ceremony in Beijing, but it was always in the context of Led Zeppelin that Page shined brightest. Just as Lennon and McCartney did their finest work as part of the Beatles, so too Page was at his zenith in Zeppelin. And strutting in front of you on the stage in 2007 he looks more "rock star" than any of the others. Wearing sunglasses and a dark trench coat, his image as the mysterious weaver of heavy-metal incantations is alive and kicking. At 1:30 into "Good Times" Page fires off the introduction to his first solo of the evening and the audience around you explodes into a deafening roar of approval. Page plays notes that are similar enough to the *Led Zeppelin* album that the crowd could sing along with the familiar passages. And the tone he uses is fuller than what his solos sound like on record. This is how Page compensates for not having any rhythm guitar parts providing accompaniment when he shifts to playing the single-note solos. You also notice that Page shifts not only the guitar tone but also his physical position. It is typical to see guitar heroes attack the front of the stage during a lead but you notice that Page actually retreats. As the concert progresses you will see him often move to a place just to the front and right (from your perspective) of Jason's drum set, where he can better feel the groove. Jones also hovers near the other side of the drums and it's an exciting thing to see the three of them working as a sympathetic and tight unit.

After Page finishes his solo he moves back toward his "station," where a sizeable floorboard of effect pedals awaits his manipulation. Now approaching the second minute of the opening song, the attention shifts back to Plant, who sings another chorus of "Good times, bad times, you know I've had my share" and the follow-up phrase, "My woman left home with a brown-eyed man but I still don't seem to care." Even though this is a first-generation hard-rock song, the connection to lyrics of the blues is clear. Plant is sharing his tale of woe but with a wink and a smile that says he feels bad for the guy who took his unfaithful girl away. At the end of this chorus (2:02), you hear Jones easily toss out a short solo that has intrigued bassists for several decades as the band moves into an ensemble jam. Page is back with his solo tone flinging out his trademark blues-scale riffs while Jones keeps the pace and Jason continues his onslaught of solid back beat interspersed with fills. Over it all Plant reminds you about the original bad-boy attitude present in rock music when he sings, "I don't care what the neighbors say; I'm gonna love you each and every day."

The original version of "Good Times" takes the lazy way out by fading the volume down over a jam on the main riff so you are intrigued to hear how Zeppelin will accommodate an ending to the live rendition being performed in front of you. The answer is Page ramping up a second solo beginning at 2:28 and lasting for twenty seconds before signaling the band to move to a pre-arranged ending. At 2:48 the entire band locks together playing the main riff four times giving Jason several wide-open beats to fill with unaccompanied drums. Page then makes eye contact with the band and they repeat the last few syncopated notes of the riff in perfect unison before pouncing on two final hits of the home power chord. Zeppelin ends "Good Times" the same way it opens, completing the circle and resulting in a frenzy all around you as the audience erupts in jubilation. You have all the information you need to feel confident that the band is in throwback excellent form and with only one song performed, the good times have just begun.

"Rock and Roll"

In 1982, the movie *Fast Times at Ridgemont High* featured the first authorized use of a Led Zeppelin song in a film. In this case it appeared only in the movie and not on the soundtrack album. Cameron Crowe, the movie's writer, had developed a relationship with Zeppelin as a young music journalist in the 1970s and was able to convince the band to allow the limited use of one song. But Crowe ended up with a different song than he wanted. In the movie, one teen male gives his friend a five-point plan for impressing a girl on a date. The fifth and most important point is that when it comes time to make out, "Whenever possible, put on side 1 of *Led Zeppelin IV*." The scene was shot before they had procured permission to use a specific song so Crowe cast his net wide by leaving any one of the four songs on that side of the album as a possibility. After the advice from the actor is given, the scene immediately cuts to the date while "Kashmir" is blasting on the car stereo. The general audience watching the movie would have chuckled at the thought that Zeppelin is the best way to put girl in the mood but all hardcore fans cry "foul" at the atrocity. "Kashmir" is not on side 1 of *Led Zeppelin IV*. Nor is it on side 2. It is the last song on side 2 of

Physical Graffiti. But that is the song Zeppelin agreed to let Crowe use and even though it didn't match the already-filmed dialogue, he didn't want to say no, and this agreement set further media uses of the Zeppelin catalog in motion.

Cameron Crowe again called on Zeppelin in 2000 to use their songs in his semi-autobiographical *Almost Famous*, which chronicles a teenage boy assigned the task of touring with an emerging hard-rock band for *Rolling Stone* magazine in the early 1970s. Having already allowed Crowe previous use of "Kashmir," the band agreed to a meeting as long as "Stairway to Heaven" was not going to be requested. Unfortunately for Crowe, that was exactly the song he wanted and he had even shot a scene in which the entire song is played uninterrupted as a means to convince the protagonist's mother that hard rock was becoming intellectual. Even though the actor in the scene incorrectly attributes the lyrics to being based on the writings of Tolkien, the sincerity of the "sales pitch" is heartfelt. Zeppelin, however, was not compelled to hand over their most valuable recording, so the scene was never used (it can be found on the Internet), but they did agree to the use of several other songs that Crowe placed tastefully in the movie.

With the wheels of commerce turning, Zeppelin saw money to be made from their back catalog and began fielding other serious offers for selected placement of songs in media. Their song "Rock and Roll" (which actually *is* on side 1 of *Led Zeppelin IV*) appeared as background music in a 2001 episode of the "Sopranos" in which the lead character is portrayed as a classic-rock-loving mob boss. But soon after, that same song became a hot topic of discussion for its placement in a car commercial.

General Motors was aggressively trying to market Cadillac to a younger demographic in 2002 when their new line of slimmed down, sport-inspired cars was ready for release. They created a campaign meant to convince car buyers (especially men) that this was "not your father's Cadillac." And the music they licensed to prove the distinction was Led Zeppelin's "Rock and Roll." The first commercial was broadcast during the 2002 Super Bowl, which was no small investment by Cadillac. The ad featured a man from a bygone decade getting on a subway and looking at a poster for the Cadillac of the day. As the rhythmic roar of the subway moving on the track builds, John Bonham's iconic drum intro to "Rock and Roll" overtakes the audio and the newer rendition of the car is revealed as Plant and company are heard doing their thing.

Cadillac sales soon rose by 16 percent so the connection to the world's most popular hard-rock band proved to be an excellent marriage and lasted in one form or another for four years. The use of the Beatles' "Revolution" by Nike in a 1987 television commercial was viewed by followers of the Fab Four as sacrilegious but by 2002 views had softened somewhat. There were a smattering of accusations that Zeppelin had "sold out" but the band turned the other cheek and cashed the checks. There is delicious irony in the fact that the band known for the most notorious, hotel-destroying, girl-deflowering, Satan-worshiping, booze-swilling debauchery in all of rock history was being paid to represent the uptown civility of the Cadillac lifestyle. While we were busy looking elsewhere, Madison Avenue went and made a lady out of a street walker. As Don Henley sang in 1984, "I saw a deadhead sticker on a Cadillac" but it would turn out to be Zeppelin, not the Grateful Dead, who endorsed the car that sticker was on.

Played as the final encore at the O2 reunion concert, "Rock and Roll" was a fitting finish to a successful concert. Aside from the musical train wreck that occurred after Page's solo in "Dazed and Confused" (Jason and Page were completely out of alignment but Jones was there to pull them back together), the first fifteen songs were strong representations of not only what the band members used to be, but also what they were at the moment: seasoned, excellent musicians who sound better playing rock and roll together rather than apart. And now, at the close of their first full concert in decades, they rewarded themselves and the audience with one of the greatest "jam" tunes in rock music.

To vent some frustration in the studio while trying to record the rhythmically challenging "Four Sticks" in 1971, Bonham broke into a drum pattern based on the introduction to "Keep a Knockin'" by Little Richard. Page and Jones joined the drummer, playing riffs not unlike the many Chuck Berry songs they knew and loved. Plant even played around with some lyrics based on oldies like "The Book of Love" and within a short amount of time the framework of a song was completed. Because of the collective input, "Rock and Roll" is one of the few Zeppelin tunes that credit all four members as songwriters. The verses of the song are relatively easy to play on guitar and bass, making it a favorite song for instrumentalists to jam to, especially if they don't know many songs together. This has unfortunately led to the myth that "Rock and Roll" is a simple song when it is not, and many bands learn the hard way when they try to cover it without enough preparation.

Standing on your feet and cheering for more music after the first encore of "Whole Lotta Love," you are optimistic the band will play at least one more. Your mind races back through the set list trying to think of what classic material they omitted that would make a good choice for the evening's last song. "When the Levee Breaks" and "You Shook Me" are too slow. "Achilles Last Stand" and "How Many More Times" are too long. "Carouselambra" and "All of My Love" are from the album Zeppelin is obviously ignoring. "Communication Breakdown," "Custard Pie," and "The Ocean" are all mid-length, up-tempo rockers that make reasonable contenders. But then Jason breaks into the open-hi-hat pattern known to all Zeppelin fans and many Cadillac owners. "Of course!" you think as you hear wild agreement from the twenty thousand souls around you. "Rock and Roll" used to be the opening song for many of Zeppelin's tours and now, at the opposite end of the band's career, it has been inverted to the final closing statement.

After the drum intro, Page and Jones jump in after four and a half measures. The two dropped beats are just one of many elements to "Rock and Roll" that make it challenging as a "jam" song but Zeppelin is no neighborhood cover band and they plow smoothly ahead to the first guitar riff. The first twelve bars are based on the oft-used blues progression and Jones keeps things simple by pounding out nothing but the root note of each chord. This harmonic anchor allows Page more freedom to play an active riff. The problem he has always faced (and placed on his imitators) during the opening of "Rock and Roll" is that on the studio version he recorded a prominent rhythm guitar part in addition to the busy riff. Translating that to a live setting where he is the only guitarist is not easy. Comparing the rendition of *Led Zeppelin IV* to what you're hearing at the O2 Arena reveals how he has made a reasonable compromise to cover both parts. Many other guitarists simply give up on the rhythm chords and play only the riff.

When the first verse begins at 0:24 Plant sings, "It's been a long time since I rock and rolled," and the audience loves the multiple meanings. Following the parlance of old R&B slang, Plant is simply referring to not having sex lately. Taken literally, it's a humorous punchline because he's been rocking all night long. Or, interpreted metaphorically, it's been many years since he rocked in the Zeppelin format and he's calling to you in the crowd to enjoy the moment with him. Each of the meanings is appropriate and you cheer for all three of them simultaneously.

Another interesting compositional element of "Rock and Roll" is that while the instrumental introduction seems to dictate the form of the song, the band deviates when the vocals enter. The blues progression played during the opening uses the standard length of twelve measures but during the lyrics the form is expanded to twenty-four measures. The academic term for this technique is *rhythmic augmentation* because they linger twice as long on each chord. But that's not on your mind as you yell out the tag "Lonely, lonely, lonely, lonely, lonely time" fifty seconds into the song. The second verse begins at 0:58 and you notice Plant is using a different melody than the original recording. This is a trick he often used even in the band's early days as a way to protect his voice when singing night after night. He had created an alternative (lower) melody and depending on how he felt during a given performance, Plant could flip between the two at will. Given the fact that the fifty-nine-year-old Plant has already been singing for two hours, it's no surprise he's taking the melodic alternate route at the O2 Arena. It also helps him that "Rock and Roll" is one of the many songs lowered in pitch on this night.

The second verse also ends with the audience-participation "lonely times" tag and then Page gears up for his final feature of the night. Beginning at 1:33, the band replays the original twelve measures used as the introduction but Page is playing looser and close to the edge. His solo begins in earnest with the twenty-four-measure form beginning at 1:50 at it's almost mayhem. Page is seen center stage with his sunburst Les Paul guitar slung low and he struts and swaggers as only he can. The light show is phenomenal and the big screen makes the four musicians larger than life. From your vantage point in the arena it's all good fun although from a pure musical standpoint Page is out of ideas. His solo is an erratic conflagration comprised of the original recording, later revisions, and his best of intentions overtaken by the fatigue of the evening. Page is cooked and leaving it all on the stage. It looks great in the hall but the guitarist isn't adding anything of great value to their complete recorded catalog. That said, Page is still playing strong enough to atone himself for the debacle of a solo he made millions of television viewers suffer through at the 1985 Live Aid concert when the

Zeppelin trio was joined by drummers Phil Collins and Tony Thompson.

During the third verse and the "ooh yeah" portion that follows, you can also hear that Plant is running on the last of his fuel as well. As a veteran rocker, he has paced himself to have just enough in the tank to get him through this final segment and he's not holding anything back. He trades measures with Page a couple of times before playfully leading you through a final few stabs at the word *lonely*. As Jason mimics the last drum solo in a brilliantly accurate John Bonham style, Plant, Page, and Jones all gravitate toward the drum set. With a nod from Jason, the guitarist and bassist strike the final chord and Plant treats the audience to one of his trademark but now seldom-heard high, wailing notes (a D). The sentimental fans in the audience fight back tears as Jason looks to the sky and touches his heart.

EPILOGUE

With the gift of hindsight, Led Zeppelin proved that their reign as the supreme rock band of the 1970s was honestly deserved and not merely the result of marketing a product to the lowest common denominator. *Led Zeppelin* remains the benchmark as one of the greatest first albums in the history of rock. The band members' bordering-on-arrogance sense of self and shockingly developed musicianship permeate every track on the album. As a result, they set the bar high not only for their future, but also for all rock bands since. Not only did they reinterpret the blues with "You Shook Me" and "I Can't Quit You Baby," but they also strut magnificently as composers of extended forms on "Dazed and Confused" and "How Many More Times." For the next twelve years they would advance but never abandon those foundational elements laid out on *Led Zeppelin*.

Then came *Led Zeppelin II*, an album recorded in such a catch-as-catch-can manner that there is no reason it should be so rip-roaring great. From "Whole Lotta Love" to "Bring It On Home" and all points in between, Zeppelin served notice that they were no fluke. They asserted themselves as a riff-based, guitar-dominated, marauding band of charming rockers. And the world welcomed them for both their craft and image. Whether improvising their way through a three-hour concert or carefully crafting an in-studio creation, Zeppelin was the complete package.

Led Zeppelin III has unfairly been labeled the "acoustic" or "folk" album in the band's catalog, which is a distinction that holds no water.

Yes, there are pastoral departures with "Friends" and "Gallows Pole," but their two previous albums each included softer moments like "Babe I'm Gonna Leave You," "Black Mountainside," and "Thank You." And how do we explain the presence of "Immigrant Song," "Celebration Day," "Out on the Tiles," and the mercurial "Since I've Been Loving You" on a folk album? Those are some of the most energetic and hardest-hitting songs heard across all the Zeppelin albums. The band was certainly flexing some of their lesser used muscles but the skeletal structure of Zeppelin was still fully intact.

And then came *Untitled*, commonly known as *Led Zeppelin IV*, which forever changed rock music with "Stairway to Heaven." Zeppelin delivered a song that had no precedent for commercial success and yet it is now impossible to envision any other outcome. The success of "Stairway" could have crushed Zeppelin into a one-song punchline, like the monster hits that had defined so many other bands. But for Zeppelin it simply filled their creative sails as they headed for deeper waters. And let us not forget that even if "Stairway" had never come to be, Zeppelin's fourth album would still have been a watershed moment with songs like "When the Levee Breaks," "Black Dog," "Going to California," and "Rock and Roll."

Their next album was *Houses of the Holy* and the question all asked was, "Is there another 'Stairway'?" There couldn't be another of course, but the band certainly rose to new heights with "The Rain Song," "No Quarter," and "The Ocean." Five albums in, and they hadn't delivered a dud yet. There was nothing that would go out of print or be abandoned to the sale bin. When fans bought a new Zeppelin album, they knew there would not just be one "hit" surrounded by tracks of useless fodder. As Zeppelin entered the second half of their recording career, they showed no sign of giving in to commercial pressures or letting their creative output suffer from internal implosions.

With fifteen songs spread across a double album, *Physical Graffiti* was Zeppelin's most adventurous release. Not only were their now-classic styles represented in songs like "Custard Pie," "The Rover," and "Sick Again," but there was also an emerging emphasis on the epic anthems that defined the latter years of Zeppelin. "Kashmir," "In the Light," and "In My Time of Dying" were game changers. The band members loved challenging themselves with material of such depth; fans loved hearing a band not willing to dumb down their material in an age of "easy listening" or "soft rock"; and radio stations loved the fact that the more they played Zeppelin the more people listened and supported advertisers. After six albums comprising fifty-nine songs, the hard-rock fandom only wanted more.

If there was any complaint to be made about *Physical Graffiti*, it was that the keyboards had taken away from the guitar work of Page. Whether or not this was a valid criticism, the band responded with *Presence*, an album featuring the stripped-down essence that made Zeppelin such a great rock band. There were no keyboards to be heard, and Page dominated more than ever with walls of guitar overdubs on rib-cracking scorchers like "Achilles Last Stand," "For Your Life," and the throwback homage "Candy Store Rock." Even though this is just the kind of album the so-called Zeppelin purists called for, strangely enough, it ended up as their least successful album in terms of sales. But to put this statistic in context, a commercially weak album for Zeppelin would have been a career-elevating success for most anyone else.

All trends tend to create their opposite, and so it was that the raw sound of *Presence* led the band toward a slicker production for the album *In Through the Out Door*. Again, we have to put this in its proper context. "Slicker" for other bands of the late 1970s usually meant drum machines and disco arrangements backed by strings and a wedge of female backup singers. For Zeppelin we're just talking about a couple of synthesizers and more tightly structured arrangements that relied less on ensemble improvisations. The album still featured several excellent guitar solos, but they do bear that sheen of pre-composed thought not present in Page's earlier work. In songs like "In the Evening," "Carouselambra," and "I'm Gonna Crawl" Jones and Plant gladly step to the forefront as writers and arrangers. Given Zeppelin's history of allowing the pendulum to swing, the band would very likely have veered back toward the guitar dominance of Page but in combination with the modern technology and orchestrations Plant and Jones were bringing into the fold. Alas, after the death of John Bonham, there was no follow-up of newly recorded material.

There was, however, the love letter to Zeppelin fans in the form of *Coda*. An album of misfits and castoffs, it comprises eight songs all worthy of release, even if the lyrics sometimes seem only first drafts in need of further polishing. "We're Gonna Groove" is as strong as any rocker from the first two albums. "Ozone Baby" and "Wearing and Tearing" are competent rockers that allow Zeppelin a platform to do what they do best. "Darlene" is a good-time swinger that pointed Plant in the direction for what would become the Honeydrippers. And Bonham was appropriately given his due in "Bonzo's Montreux." *Coda* is not rich with songs representing Zeppelin at their crest, but it is a fine showing of what they had left, and frankly that's better than most.

ACCOLADES FOR LED ZEPPELIN

Zeppelin has attracted generations of fans born too late to experience the band's active years. It's hard for music enthusiasts of that age to contemplate a society that didn't always shower rock stars and controversial pop icons with awards, but such strange days did once exist. And so it is that Zeppelin never won a Grammy award during their twelve-year run. The closest they came to a performance-related Grammy was a nomination for "New Artist" in 1970, but the award went to Crosby, Stills & Nash. In the early 1970s the Grammys for categories like Rock, Hard Rock, and certainly "Metal" were still many years away from existence. The one area a rock band could slip through the cracks had nothing to do with music. Zeppelin did just that and was nominated for "Best Album Package" in 1974 (*Houses of the Holy*), 1976 (*Physical Graffiti*), 1977 (*Presence*), and for the fourth time in 1980 (*In Through the Out Door*). They didn't win any of those Grammys either. Zeppelin at the Grammy Awards was like the bad-boy boyfriend a daughter brings to Thanksgiving dinner while everyone else scrambles to hide the family jewels.

But numbers don't lie, and the industry that originally ignored bands like Zeppelin, Pink Floyd, and Black Sabbath eventually learned how to worship at their collective feet. The Zeppelin catalog is one of the most valuable on the planet, making Page, Plant, and Jones three very wealthy individuals indeed. Their worldwide sales are over 250 million (some say 300 million), which puts them in the top seven highest-selling acts of all time. In the United States, Zeppelin has over 100 million certified sales, second to only one other band—the Beatles—and fourth among all artists, behind only the Beatles, Elvis Presley, and Garth Brooks. Zeppelin's most successful record is *Led Zeppelin IV*, one of the ten best-selling albums worldwide, with 29 million certified sales and an unverified claim of 37 million. In the United States, *Led Zeppelin IV* is the third best-selling album of all time, with 23 million certified sales—behind *Thriller* by Michael Jackson and *Their Greatest Hits (1971–1975)* by the Eagles. And all this from a band that had to finance their own first album and shop for a record deal after the fact.

As the years of the 1980s and 1990s rolled on, it became clear that the Zeppelin catalog showed no signs of waning popularity. As CDs became popular, record companies repackaged back catalogs as cheaply as possible to satisfy the emerging "digital" market. Page was mortified at the quality of the first generation of Zeppelin CDs and set to work remastering the studio recordings. Released in 1990, the *Led Zeppelin Boxed Set* broke all records for the sales of a CD set and further fueled record companies to repackage music from the archives rather than spend money on risky new bands. So called "dinosaurs" like Zeppelin were record industry cash cows.

The mid-1990s teased Zeppelin fans with a two-album project between Page and Plant that included a worldwide tour. Their first album, *Unledded*, rose to number 4 on the Billboard Top 200 chart and has verified platinum sales status (over 1 million sales), proving that anything Zeppelin-like still had considerable commercial value. The second album, *Walking into Clarksdale*, was released in 1998 and reached number 8 on the Billboard Top 200 while the song "Most High" hit number 1 on the Billboard Mainstream Rock chart and went on to win a Grammy. By 1998, long hair and distorted guitars had become acceptable enough to warrant an appropriate category at the Grammy Awards and Page-Plant finally received recognition not available to them in the Zeppelin years when "Most High" won for "Best Hard Rock Performance."

Another way Grammy Awards were handed out to artists who missed out earlier in their career was through the creation of the Grammy Hall of Fame. This allowed sponsors of the Grammy to paper over past mistakes by giving awards to musicians for creative output that history had revealed worthy over time—something the rest of us seemed to know all along. Led Zeppelin received four such honors for either albums or songs: *Led Zeppelin IV* (1999); "Stairway to Heaven" (2003); *Led Zeppelin* (2004); and "Whole Lotta Love" (2008). If this wasn't enough, the Grammy Awards found one more way to atone for their previous Zeppelin snubbing, specifically by giving them a "Life-time Achievement Award" in 2005. This should have closed the book on Zeppelin's "mercy" Grammys, but along came *Celebration Day* and the band earned their first-ever performance Grammy for Best Rock Album in 2014. To their credit, no one from the band attended the ceremony, and hostess Cindy Lauper offered awkward appreciation in their absence.

Zeppelin did, however, attend a fabulous evening of accolades December 2, 2012. Page, Plant, and Jones were honored for their contribution to American culture and the arts by a White House dinner and formal ceremony at the Kennedy Center. In his special comments, President Obama aptly described each musician and their collective impression on the American public:

> There was this singer with a mane like a lion and a voice like a banshee, a guitar prodigy who left people's jaws on the floor, a versatile bassist who was equally at home on the keyboards, a drummer who played like his life depended on it. . . . And when the Brits initially kept their distance, Led Zeppelin grabbed America from the opening chord. We were ready for what Jimmy called songs with "a lot of light and shade."

The Kennedy Center Honors concluded with a Led Zeppelin tribute concert featuring exceptional performances and a spirited narrative from actor Jack Black. The Foo Fighters (with Dave Grohl on drums as he had played in Them Crooked Vultures with Jones) gave credible renditions of "Black Dog" and "Rock and Roll." The vocals of Taylor Hawkins were shaky at times but singing Zeppelin classics under the watchful eyes of Plant in the balcony is no easy assignment. Kid Rock and Lenny Kravitz more convincingly offered their contributions, but the finale by sisters Ann and Nancy Wilson was a tremendous climax to the event. As members of Heart, the Zeppelin-loving Wilsons have performed "Stairway to Heaven" many times but took matters more seriously for this occasion. With Jason Bonham on drums, the song started off in the usual fashion and got more interesting when a small vocal group came out to add harmonies. But as the song progressed into the section with the faster tempo (see "A Closer Look" in chapter 4), a back curtain rose to reveal an enormous gospel choir all wearing bowler hats in tribute to John Bonham. Jones and Page were visibly taken aback by the spectacle, and even Plant, who has often expressed his detachment from "Stairway," watched with moistened eyes and an approving smile.

The next night, Led Zeppelin appeared on *The David Letterman Show* (Letterman, another Kennedy Center Honoree, had sat next to the band throughout the ceremony) to comment on the event. In a playful but poignant moment, Letterman first displayed a picture of the group (now all in their sixties) being greeted by the president of the United States and then jumping to a classic photo of all four band members standing in front of their own jet airliner as young lions of rock. With both Plant and Jones pictured with bare chests, Letterman quipped how the flight must have been "shirts optional." Letterman was keen on pointing out the irony that a band known for depraving American youth, smashing hotel rooms, and generally flaunting rockstar excess could survive the decades and rise to a prominence in which world leaders shake their hands and say, "Thank you for your contribution to our society." It's been a long, strange trip, to be sure.

THE FUTURE OF LED ZEPPELIN

In a rare television interview on "Midnight Special" from 1975, Plant responded to a question about Zeppelin's future plans from Los Angeles disc jockey (and future MTV host) J. J. Jackson:

> I am totally at peace with myself when I'm involved 100% in what I'm doing as of this moment. And providing that I can maintain that peace of mind with the other three members of the group, then I believe that the guys who dug us when they are at my age may still be following us along at fifty if we keep moving in a reasonable way. I don't see that there should be any time to stop.

These prophetic words from Plant still apply long after he and his original fan base passed their fifties and even sixties. At the time, all members of Zeppelin saw "100%" as a reasonable level of commitment, but that threshold would prove unsustainable and in the case of Plant, unrealistic, especially when the primary question to haunt their steps is, "Will there be more?"

The question remains valid but the answer is difficult for all parties. Jones and Page have long shown a willingness to rekindle the brand. There was considerable chatter just after the 2007 concert at the O2 Arena that a tour would follow. And at the time it made perfect sense. A two-hour show had been rehearsed and produced with all the trappings of lights, sound, staging, and video. The time-sucking groundwork was laid, making further performances the same year more economical for all concerned. So what happened? Plant had an unplanned hit record with Alison Krauss, and he suddenly felt that Zeppelin wasn't as young and pretty as this new musical mistress. Looking at the situation from his perspective, he made a choice between struggling night after night to sing songs that no longer felt relevant to him, or performing cool, acoustically based Americana and hanging out in Nashville with a new crowd that included super-producer T-bone Burnett.

Meanwhile, Page and Jones kept Jason Bonham at the ready and even went so far as to work with new singers. Secret rehearsals (that weren't well kept) with Aerosmith's Steve Tyler produced no results. And as intriguing as collaboration with Myles Kennedy from Alter Bridge sounds on paper, nothing happened there either. With such experienced and excellent talent to pick from, what more were Jones and Page looking for? They may have been playing a bluff hoping to lure a jealous Plant back to the band, but it didn't work. Plant ended up making a second album in Nashville, and the prospect of Zeppelin with a new singer never gained enough traction. The drum chair may be flexible (although Jason has certainly proved his worth), but without the three surviving members all involved, Led Zeppelin does not function properly.

And who can really blame Plant for balking at a full tour? Even at the age of fifty-nine in 2007 he had to lower the song keys for most of the show. New melodies were created to cover his changed voice, and he felt little or no connection to some lyrics the audience (and the other band members) expected him to sing. True, he managed to pull it off on one night, but now, years later, a full tour would add very little to his legacy while putting much of it at risk. Robert Plant is still a great singer, but he is not the vocalist he was, nor should we ask him to be. Most vocalists of his generation are experiencing the same problems, and sometimes worse. Sammy Hagar, David Coverdale, and Glenn Hughes have maintained their vocal health (and in the case of Hughes, actually improved with age) but they are the exceptions not the rule. Roger Daltrey, Ian Gillan, David Lee Roth, and Axl Rose have all painfully tried to keep singing their early hits, and the effort has not done their reputations much good. And unlike some old-school rockers, Plant doesn't need the money or the fame; he has lots of both. So if he ever comes around to wanting to give Zeppelin another go, fans everywhere will no doubt rejoice. But should he opt to just ramble on down the road, let's give the man a break and find enjoyment in the many classic records he made for us.

As for Jones, he soldiers on creating and producing music of various genres that he finds agreeable. He toured behind two exceedingly well-crafted solo albums in which he made good use of stringed instruments most fans at his shows didn't know existed. He also found an incredibly creative home in the company of David Grohl (Nirvana, Foo Fighters) and Josh Homme (Kyuss, Queens of the Stone Age). Their "super group" released an excellent album under the name "Them Crooked Vultures" and has promised more material in the future. Although he was forever the "quiet" member of Zeppelin, Jones has revealed himself to be immensely humorous and at times sanguine about his status as a living legend. To better appreciate his sense of satire, listen to the song "Angry Angry" from his *Thunderthief* album in which he shows that he is more than capable of having a laugh at himself. He has even delivered subtle but well-aimed blows at Plant and Page, who have occasionally teamed up without his services. At the 1995 induction ceremony for the Rock and Roll Hall of Fame, Plant gave a wandering six-minute speech to which Jones followed up by simply acknowledging Peter Grant and then with a quick look at his band mates added, "Thank you my friends for finally remembering my phone number." Plant was visibly not amused. But Jones's cheekiness has not festered into deep resentment, and it is clear he would relearn the old songs when the phone call comes.

As for Page, he is the one of the three who seems the most lost when Zeppelin is not active. Plant has over a dozen post-Zeppelin albums to his credit while Page has only produced five (two with the Firm, one with David Coverdale, one solo album, and a live concert with the Black Crowes). He consistently revisits the aging Zeppelin catalog in various mastering and re-release projects. For Page, Zeppelin became so embedded in his musical and spiritual identity that there seems to be no other worthy avenue for him to pursue. While he has dated and even married other rock-and-roll courtesans, Zeppelin has proved to be the great love of his life and without her, he drifts among the less meaningful shadows looking for a glimpse of past light.

Led Zeppelin may not ever make new music again, but their brilliant recorded catalog is always available to us anytime we want to feel the swagger, darkness, and brilliance that defined the band's essence and an entire genre of rock music. To borrow a sentiment from the great composer Duke Ellington, there are two kinds of music: good and bad. Led Zeppelin made the good kind.

SELECTED READINGS

Carruthers, Bob. *Led Zeppelin: Uncensored on the Record*. Warwickshire, England: Coda Books, 2011. Carruthers emphasizes the use of primary sources whenever possible. The writing style is conversational, and Carruthers certainly knows the subject matter. The work includes lengthy first-person accounts from journalists who toured with Led Zeppelin.

Lewis, David. *Led Zeppelin: The Complete Guide to Their Music*. London: Omnibus Press, 2004. Lewis knows his topic as well as anyone and his guide is the go-to source for all basic Led Zeppelin scholarship. A revised edition with the 2007 reunion concert is needed.

Rees, Paul. *Robert Plant: A Life*. New York: It Books, 2013. Rees's biography is credited as the "definitive" biography of Plant, but that is simply because there is no other. Rees has culled from existing interviews and articles to thread together a narrative and until Plant or others near to him begin opening up, this will have to serve as the single book-length source on the singer's life.

Somach, Denny, and Carol Miller. *Get the Led Out: How Led Zeppelin Became the Biggest Band in the World*. New York: Sterling, 2012. This work includes a comprehensive day-by-day calendar of the band's activities. It also includes many images of memorabilia not found elsewhere, as well as exclusive interviews of key figures and musicians of the era. A very useful resource.

Wall, Mick. *When Giants Walked the Earth: A Biography of Led Zeppelin*. New York: St. Martin's Press, 2010. Mick Wall must have been a fly on the wall to have gotten all the inside information for this book. He includes quotes and facts that no one should have without having been in the room when it happened or knowing someone who was. An impressive offering.

———. *Led Zeppelin Dazed and Confused: The Stories behind Every Song*. New York: Thunder's Mouth Press, 1998. As with his *When Giants Walked the Earth*, Wall has an enormous amount of insider information about the making of Led Zeppelin's music. Unfortunately, the material is outdated because of new revelations and recent scholarship.

Welch, Chris. *Peter Grant: The Man Who Led Zeppelin*. London: Omnibus Press, 2002. Welch has done the legacy of Peter Grant a service by working mightily to get the story right in what will likely be the only biography ever written about Led Zeppelin's manager. The many exclusive interviews, along with support from Grant family members and personal accounts of the author, make this an insightful and well-written resource.

SELECTED LISTENING

STUDIO ALBUMS

Led Zeppelin released January 12, 1969, Atlantic Records.
Led Zeppelin II released October 22, 1969, Atlantic Records.
Led Zeppelin III released October 5, 1970, Atlantic Records.
Untitled (Led Zeppelin IV) released November 8, 1971, Atlantic Records.
Houses of the Holy released March 28, 1973, Atlantic Records.
Physical Graffiti released February 24, 1975, Swan Song Records.
Presence released March 31, 1976, Swan Song Records.
In Through the Out Door released August 15, 1979, Swan Song Records.
Coda released November 19, 1982, Swan Song Records.

LIVE ALBUMS

The Song Remains the Same released October 22, 1976, Swan Song Records.
BBC Sessions released November 11, 1997, Atlantic Records.
How the West Was Won released May 27, 2003, Atlantic Records.
Celebration Day released November 19, 2012, Atlantic Records.

FILM/DVD

The Song Remains the Same released October 20, 1976, Warner
    Brothers.
Led Zeppelin released May 26, 2003, Atlantic Records.
Celebration Day released November 19, 2012, Atlantic Records.

INDEX

ABOUT THE AUTHOR

Gregg Akkerman is a writer/performer/educator born in the southern California desert to a mother with the good sense to provide her son the same birthday as Duke Ellington. He worked many years as a pianist/vocalist throughout the Southwest before earning a Masters of Music from San Diego State University and a Doctorate of Arts from the University of Northern Colorado. His first book, *The Last Balladeer: The Johnny Hartman Story*, was published in 2012 and Akkerman also serves as editor of *The Listener's Companion* book series from Rowman & Littlefield. Akkerman served as a tenured professor of music for nine years before leaving academia to focus more on writing and private instruction. Currently residing in San Diego, he still performs regularly and specializes in rock music and the Great American Songbook.